—African-American Biographies—

BETTY SHABAZZ

Sharing the Vision of Malcolm X

Series Consultant:
Dr. Russell L. Adams, Chairman
Department of Afro-American Studies, Howard University

Laura S. Jeffrey

Enslow Publishers, Inc.

40 Industrial Road	PO Box 38
Box 398	Aldershot
Berkeley Heights, NJ 07922	Hants GU12 6BP
USA	UK

http://www.enslow.com

Library of Congress Cataloging-in-Publication Data

Jeffrey, Laura S.
    Betty Shabazz : sharing the vision of Malcolm X / Laura S. Jeffrey.
        p. cm. — (African-American biographies)
Includes bibliographical references and index.
Summary: Profiles the life of Betty Shabazz, the widow of Malcolm X, discussing her life
as the wife of the outspoken civil rights leader and her role in the civil rights movement
after his death.
    ISBN 0-7660-1210-7
    1. Shabazz, Betty—Juvenile literature. 2. X, Malcolm, 1925–1965—Juvenile literature.
3. Black Muslims—Biography—Juvenile literature. [1. Shabazz, Betty. 2. X, Malcolm,
1925–1965. 3. Afro-Americans—Biography. 4. Women—Biography. 5. Black Muslims.]
I. Title. II. Series.
    BP223.Z8 J44 2000
    320.54'092—dc21
                                                                          99-050847

Printed in the United States of America

10 9 8 7 6 5 4 3 2 1

To Our Readers:
All Internet addresses in this book were active and appropriate when we went to press.
Any comments or suggestions can be sent by e-mail to Comments@enslow.com or to the
address on the back cover.

Illustration Credits:
© *Washington Post*; reprinted by permission of the D.C. Public Library, p. 47;
Anthony Mills, p. 4; Associated Press, pp. 66, 104; Brian Lanker photo, cour-
tesy of Ilyasah Shabazz, p. 109; Courtesy of Gamilah-Lamumba Shabazz, pp.
13, 18, 79; Courtesy of Ilyasah Shabazz, p. 69; Michael Ochs Archives/Venice,
CA, p. 38; Photofest, p. 88; Reproduced from the Collections of the Library of
Congress, pp. 8, 15, 25, 34, 57, 61, 83; Richard Saunders courtesy of the
Schomburg Center for Research in Black Culture, by permission of the Estate
of Betty Shabazz, p. 44; Robert L. Haggins, pp. 49, 54; Royal Embassy of Saudi
Arabia, Information Office, p. 70; The Schomburg Center for Research in
Black Culture, by permission of the Estate of Betty Shabazz, pp. 28, 57.

Cover Illustration: Anthony Mills

Contents

Betty Shabazz, with a photo of Malcolm X in the background.

1

SUDDENLY
WIDOWED

etty Shabazz bundled herself and her four young daughters into their winter coats and stepped outside into the bitter cold day. It was February 21, 1965. Betty and the children were headed to the Audubon Ballroom in Harlem, a neighborhood of New York City. There, Betty's husband, El-Hajj Malik El-Shabazz, was going to give a lecture. He was a controversial human rights leader who had formerly been known as Malcolm X. Betty's husband had been the top spokesman for the Nation of Islam. This group was led by Elijah Muhammad, who called himself the messenger of God. Members of the Nation of Islam believed that black people were superior to white people and that white people had been created by a black scientist. Following Muhammad's teachings, Malcolm X called white people "devils." He supported segregation of the black and white races.

With these views, Malcolm X had become a very controversial public figure. He was feared by many white people and by many black people as well. Yet Malcolm X was also greatly admired. He preached self-sufficiency for African Americans and frowned on drug and alcohol use. He received a lot of publicity and persuaded many people to join the Nation of Islam.

On that February day, however, Malcolm no longer represented the Nation of Islam. Almost a year earlier, he had learned of financial and moral wrongdoings committed by Elijah Muhammad. Malcolm had left the Nation of Islam. He took a pilgrimage, or spiritual journey, to Africa and the Middle East, returning with a new religion and a new name. Malcolm had changed his views, too. He now believed it was possible for blacks and whites to live together in peace. Betty also left the Nation of Islam. She embraced her husband's new beliefs.

The changes in Malcolm's views, and his unwavering moral stance, angered many Nation of Islam members. They threatened to kill him. Days before the speech at the ballroom, Malcolm and Betty's home in

East Elmhurst, New York, had been firebombed. Betty and the children moved in with a friend, and Malcolm checked into a hotel. Malcolm feared for his family's safety. He did not want to endanger them by living with them.

Malcolm told his family not to attend his lecture at the Audubon Ballroom, so Betty had not planned to go hear her husband speak that February day. At the last minute, however, Malcolm called Betty. He asked her to come and bring the children with her. Excited, Betty agreed. When she arrived at the ballroom, she and the children settled on seats near the front of the stage where Malcolm was to speak.

Shortly after 2:00 P.M., Malcolm came out and greeted the audience. About five hundred people were there. As he began his lecture, a scuffle broke out in the back of the ballroom. The audience turned to look, and Malcolm asked everyone to stay calm. Suddenly, some men in the front row stood up. They pulled out guns and started shooting.

As soon as Betty heard the shots, she threw the children onto the floor. Then she covered them with her own body. Meanwhile, the crowd panicked. People screamed, cried, shouted for help, and ran to the stage. Betty looked up, but in the confusion she could not see her husband. She got up and fought her way through the crowd. "My husband!" she screamed. "They're killing my husband!"[1]

Betty finally got to Malcolm, but it was too late. Her husband of seven years lay on the floor. Malcolm, at the age of thirty-nine, was dead from several gunshot wounds. Betty, just thirty years old, was pregnant with twins. In one horrible moment, she had become a widow who would soon have six children to raise on her own.

"She could have gone into permanent mourning and the world would have understood," New York congressman Charles Rangel said many years later.[2] But

Here in the Audubon Ballroom in Harlem, New York, Betty Shabazz witnessed the brutal murder of her husband, Malcolm X.

Betty Shabazz did not do that. After her husband's death, she became a leader in her own right. As a colleague and friend noted, "Her perpetuation of Malcolm's vision grew by leaps and bounds throughout the years."[3]

Betty Shabazz raised her and Malcolm's daughters. She furthered her education. She went to work full-time and became actively involved in many organizations promoting civil and human rights. Courage and strength were the words most often associated with her. Shabazz became a major role model in the African-American community. Only her desire for privacy and tendency to avoid publicity prevented her from becoming as well known and widely admired in the white community as well. Her life was tragically cut short on June 23, 1997, three weeks after she was severely burned in a house fire.

Shabazz received many honors during her life as well as after her untimely death. Her six daughters, now grown, have taken turns accepting the awards and speaking on behalf of their beloved mother. Their sorrow has been eased when they realize how much their mother accomplished, and how many lives she touched.

Gamilah-Lamumba Shabazz, the fourth-born child, remembered the days when her mother was in the hospital, desperately trying to recover from the painful burns that eventually took her life. "She received almost five thousand cards from everyone from kindergartners to senior citizens," Gamilah-Lamumba said. "And people were flocking from all over."[4] Visitors included Coretta Scott King, the widow of Martin Luther King, Jr.; poet Maya Angelou; New York mayor David Dinkins; and former mayor Ed Koch. President Clinton sent a message with wishes and prayers for Shabazz's recovery.

"And then it just hit us, 'My God, they're not here because she's Malcolm X's wife,'" Gamilah-Lamumba added. "They're here because she's Betty Shabazz."[5]

Who was Betty Shabazz? In many ways, she was a simple woman performing simple acts of kindness and love. Yet her accomplishments were much greater considering the pain she endured, the hatred and fear she encountered, and the struggles she faced. For others, it probably would have taken a huge effort just to make it through each day. Yet Betty Shabazz lived her life not only with courage and strength but also with spirit. Here is her story.

2

A SHELTERED CHILDHOOD

etty Shabazz was born Betty Dean Sanders on May 28, 1934, in Pinehurst, Georgia. When she was an infant, Betty lived with her grandmother, Matilda Greene, and an aunt in Georgia. Her aunt died when Betty was about six years old. Betty then went to live with her biological mother, Ollie, in Detroit. By that time, Betty's mother had a husband and other children. Because Betty Shabazz was such a private person, few details are available about her childhood. But according to her third-born daughter, Ilyasah, her mother's life was unsettled in its earliest years.

When Betty was about twelve years old, she began baby-sitting for a middle-class African-American family in Detroit. Lorenzo Don Malloy, a college graduate, owned his own shoe-repair shop. His wife, Helen Malloy, was a schoolteacher. She also was very involved with Bethel A.M.E. (African Methodist Episcopal) Church. "They fell in love" with Betty, Ilyasah said. "So they informally adopted her."[1]

With the Malloys, Betty found love, comfort, and security. "It was the Malloy family who really instilled all the values that my mother possessed," Ilyasah recalled. "While she loved and obtained a solid relationship with her natural parents, Shelman and Ollie, she regarded Helen and Lorenzo Malloy as her true parents."[2] Under their guidance, Betty flourished.

The Malloys had established a fairly comfortable lifestyle despite the Great Depression, which began in October 1929. During this time, stock market prices fell steeply. Thousands of banks and businesses failed. As a result, millions of people were unemployed and lost their life savings.

World War II (1939–1945) brought an end to the Great Depression. The war created jobs, and millions of Americans went to work in factories or joined the United States military. Yet just as much of American society was segregated, so too was the military. At the beginning of the war, the Marine Corps did not allow African Americans to join. The Navy admitted blacks

Betty's father, Shelman Sanders (nicknamed Juju), and grandmother, Matilda Greene. Despite being informally adopted by the Malloys, Betty stayed close to her biological family.

but allowed them to work only in food-service jobs. The Army also restricted the number of African Americans who could join.

As the war progressed and the need for men and women became critical, more and more jobs opened to African Americans. These servicemen were usually placed in segregated units, but they proved they were as capable as white men.

Although Americans were supposed to be united against Germany, Japan, and other countries that supported them, African-American soldiers were often treated poorly by the white soldiers. Several years after the war, the famous African-American writer James Baldwin described the situation in an article for *The New Yorker* magazine. He wrote of black soldiers overseas not being allowed in servicemen's clubs when whites were dancing, of being forced to eat and drink in separate facilities, and receiving less respect than the German prisoners of war. For Baldwin and other African Americans, this was demoralizing.

"I was . . . assured that what had happened to the Jews in Germany could not happen to the Negroes in America," Baldwin wrote, "but I thought, bleakly, that the German Jews had probably believed similar counsellors."[3]

Back in the United States, race riots sometimes erupted. In 1942, blacks and whites had clashed in Betty's hometown of Detroit when the first African-American families moved into an all-white housing project. Yet Detroit was more integrated than many American cities and had several businesses owned by African Americans. After the war, thousands of African-American soldiers returned to towns with separate schools, shops, restaurants, and restrooms, and with limited chances of finding meaningful employment. Their frustration formed part of the foundation for the social unrest that was to come in the 1950s.

Betty's mother helped organize protests against stores in Detroit that would not hire African Americans. Still, in the Malloy house, racial issues were generally not topics of conversation.

Betty herself said years later that she was unaware of problems in her hometown. "It was hoped that by denying the existence of race problems, the problems would go away," she once wrote. "Anyone who openly

Betty spent her childhood years in the city of Detroit, Michigan, pictured above in 1942.

discussed racial relations was quickly viewed as a 'troublemaker.'"[4]

Trouble was not a word associated with Betty Sanders. After coming to live with the Malloys, her days were filled with typical childhood activities. She went to dances and movies with her friends. She attended Bethel A.M.E. Church every Sunday, where she sang in the youth choir.

"She was Miss Goody Two-Shoes, what you would call the good girl in the class," her daughter Gamilah-Lamumba said. "If she went to a party, she never smoked and she never drank. She always did well. She always did what she was supposed to do."[5]

"Pick a week out of my life. If you understood that week, you understood my life," Betty once said. "I went to school from Monday to Friday. On Friday I went to the movies. On Saturday I was at my parents' store. On Sunday I went to church. Sometimes on Saturday I would go with the young people from church to parties.

"I had been adopted by older persons, and their one agenda for me was that I should be happy," Betty added. "If I wanted a new dress or whatever, I got it."[6]

Betty attended Northern High School, where she joined a social group called the Del Sprites. She earned good grades and had many friends, both black and white. She played snare drums in the school orchestra and joined the nursing club and the French club.

A classmate recalled her as quiet, eager, and unassuming. "There were boys at the church that she liked and there were boys at her school that she liked," recalled a childhood friend, Suesetta McCree. "But she wasn't a little chatterbox about boys. She talked about other girls, but not in a jealous way. She talked about . . . what they were doing, but it was not gossipy."[7]

"She'd come over to my house, and we used to bake cookies and listen to records," McCree added. "She did a real interesting dance where everything moved. It was like she was on a string; all her joints moved."[8]

At home, Betty's father often spoke about how his

education had enabled him to buy a house and own a business. "My father felt that if he could profit from an education, others could as well," Betty once said.[9] Naturally, then, Betty would go to college. She thought she might like to be a teacher.

After Betty graduated from high school in 1952, she began classes at Tuskegee Institute in Alabama. Her adoptive mother and father had also attended this historically African-American college. Here, deep in the heart of the South and away from her protective parents, Betty had her first personal encounters with racism. The details are lost to history but in later years, Betty simply spoke of "hostilities and irritation" between blacks and whites.

"Her parents wanted her to ignore [the racism] as just something that happens," said her daughter Ilyasah.[10] "The South was the South," daughter Gamilah-Lamumba added. "It was a dangerous time back then."[11]

After a year at Tuskegee, Betty decided to change career paths. She wanted to become a nurse. A guidance counselor at Tuskegee suggested that Betty apply to New York's Brooklyn State Hospital School of Nursing, which was affiliated with Tuskegee. Betty's parents supported the move.

"My mother was such a good daughter that I don't think they really worried about her," Ilyasah said. "Her morals were in place, her values, her standards. She was an excellent child."[12]

Betty gave this 1952 Northern High School graduation photo to her grandparents.

After two years at Tuskegee, Betty left Alabama and headed north to Brooklyn to work toward her certification as a registered nurse. Moving to New York would prove to be the most significant decision of her life. While Betty had been enjoying high school and studying at Tuskegee, a fiery preacher for the Nation of Islam was making a name for himself. His name was Malcolm X, and he was speaking out against racism and spreading the teachings of Elijah Muhammad. His harsh words on racial separation frightened many white people and some African Americans, too.

Malcolm X had once lived in Detroit, but he and Betty had not crossed paths there. Instead, they would meet in New York, both as adults, with life experiences that enabled them to understand and learn from each other. Then, for the first time in her life, "Miss Goody Two-Shoes" would defy her parents' wishes.

3

MALCOLM X

he world came to know and remember him as Malcolm X. The year before he died, he was given the Muslim name El-Hajj Malik El-Shabazz. He came into the world as Malcolm Little, born on May 19, 1925, in Omaha, Nebraska. Malcolm was the fourth of eight children. His parents were the Reverend Earl Little and Earl's second wife, Louise Norton, who was from the West Indies. She had a very light complexion and was sometimes mistaken for a white woman.

Turmoil and controversy surrounded Malcolm from an early age. His father, the Reverend Earl Little, was trained as a Baptist minister. However, he spent much of his time spreading the views of a close friend, the black nationalist Marcus Garvey. Garvey, a Jamaican, came to America in 1916 and settled in Harlem in New York City. In 1917, the United States had entered World War I (1914–1918), and the mood of the country was unsettled. Also, race riots had broken out in some cities. Garvey was motivated to establish a chapter of the Universal Negro Improvement Association (UNIA), which he had begun in Jamaica. Louise Little served as the chapter's recording secretary.

Garvey believed that black people should return to Africa because they would never find in America the freedom, independence, and self-respect they deserved.[1] By 1920, the UNIA had hundreds of chapters all over the world. Still, not all African Americans of the day agreed with Garvey's views. The dissenters included black leaders W. E. B. Du Bois and A. Philip Randolph.

Du Bois was a highly educated teacher and author. He was one of the founders of the National Association for the Advancement of Colored People (NAACP). Randolph, another early civil rights leader, urged African Americans not to fight for America during World War I because they had not truly achieved equality on their own soil. Randolph was arrested for his statements but later released. Randolph continued his activism. He would go on to become an important figure in the American labor movement. He also helped organize the March on Washington in August 1963, where the Reverend Martin Luther King, Jr., delivered his stirring "I Have a Dream" speech.

Garvey was imprisoned on mail-fraud charges in 1922. Five years later, he was deported to Jamaica. His movement in the United States faltered, but Earl Little was among a few people who continued to deliver Garvey's message. This caused trouble for the Little family. Shortly after Malcolm was born, the Littles moved from Omaha to Milwaukee, Wisconsin. Then, after whites threatened him, Earl Little moved his family to Lansing, Michigan. Malcolm was three years old. In Lansing, the Littles' home was set on fire.

In September 1931, when Malcolm was six years old, his father was killed. The circumstances were never verified, but Malcolm and his family believed that Earl Little died after he was beaten by a group of white men and thrown under a trolley.[2] Louise Little was left to raise her large family on her own.

Life for the Little family began to deteriorate. Six years after his father died, Malcolm's mother was condemned by the courts to be mentally unstable. She was hospitalized for mental illness, so Malcolm and his siblings were scattered to foster families.

Malcolm was sent to live with a family in Michigan. Finally, his life seemed to be turning around. Even when he was a little boy, Malcolm's parents had encouraged reading. Now, in junior high, Malcolm did well in school and even was elected class president in the eighth grade. By the next year, however, he was frustrated and disillusioned.

"They didn't have too many Negro doctors or lawyers, especially where I grew up," Malcolm once said. "They didn't even have any Negro firemen. . . . When I was a youth, the only thing you could dream about becoming was a good waiter or a good busboy or a good shoeshine man."[3]

One day, a white teacher asked Malcolm what he planned to do with his life. Malcolm said he was thinking about becoming a lawyer. The teacher discouraged him, saying that African Americans were more suited to menial jobs. "I just gave up," Malcolm recalled.[4] He left school after the eighth grade and never returned. He went to live in Boston with an older half-sister, Ella Collins.

There, Malcolm was largely on his own. He held a series of odd jobs to earn money. They included shining shoes at a jazz club, working as a soda-fountain clerk in a drugstore, clearing tables in a restaurant, and working at a railroad yard. The railroad job enabled Malcolm to travel back and forth between Boston and New York. In both cities, Malcolm found trouble. He pretended he was mentally unstable to avoid being drafted into the Army during World War II (1939–1945). Over the next few years he started taking drugs and selling them, burglarizing homes, and robbing people.[5]

In 1946, Malcolm was arrested for his role in a burglary. He was sentenced to ten years in prison and began serving his term in Massachusetts. To pass the time, Malcolm read a variety of newspapers, magazines, and books. He continued his education with a correspondence course in Latin, and he read biographies and books about history and philosophy. He also wrote letters to his family.

Through his older siblings, Malcolm learned of a man in Chicago named Elijah Muhammad. Muhammad, who called himself the messenger of Allah (the Arabic word for God), was the leader of a religious group called the Nation of Islam. Followers of the Nation of Islam were called Black Muslims. Two of Malcolm's brothers had already become Black Muslims.

Muhammad taught his followers that the white race was created to run hell, which existed on earth. White people were devils, according to Muhammad, while black people were God's chosen ones. Because of his own experiences, Malcolm wholeheartedly embraced these concepts.

"Every white man in America, when he looks into a black man's eyes, should fall to his knees and say, 'I'm sorry, I'm sorry—my kind has committed history's greatest crime against your kind; will you give me the

Elijah Muhammad, religious leader of the Nation of Islam, delivers a stirring speech to a crowd of Black Muslim followers.

chance to atone?'" Malcolm once said. "But do you brothers and sisters expect any white man to do that? *No*, you *know* better! And why won't he do it? Because he *can't* do it. The white man has *created* a devil, to bring chaos upon this earth."[6]

The Black Muslims followed very strict rules of conduct. They were not allowed to drink, smoke, use drugs, or engage in promiscuous behavior. Even casual dating was frowned upon. Black Muslims were not allowed to eat pork and were encouraged to eat only one meal a day. They could not attend dances, watch movies or ball games, or sleep late.

Black Muslims also used "X" as their last name. The X represented the loss of their original names to slavery. "These so-called Negroes in this country who have these names like Johnson, Jones, Smith, Powell and Bunche . . . actually are wearing the names of their slave masters, not the names of their forefathers," Malcolm later said.[7]

While he was in prison, Malcolm began following the Islam religion. He also wrote letters to Muhammad, who wrote back, explaining more about his beliefs. In 1952, the same year that Betty Sanders graduated from high school, Malcolm was released from prison. He officially became Malcolm X. He was in his late twenties.

Malcolm moved to Detroit and went to work, first in a factory and then on the assembly line of an automobile manufacturer. He attended a Nation of Islam temple there, and he visited Muhammad in Chicago. Muhammad recognized Malcolm's talents. Observing the strength of Malcolm's beliefs and leadership abilities, Muhammad took a special interest in the younger man. Muhammad personally tutored Malcolm on the ways of Islam, preparing him to spread the word.

Eventually, Malcolm quit his job so that he could devote all of his time to the Nation of Islam. By the summer of 1953, Malcolm was named assistant minister of Detroit Temple No. 1. He was soon promoted to organizing temples in Boston and Philadelphia.

At the time Malcolm X was moving up in the Black Muslim ranks, American society continued to be largely segregated. The American courts had ruled that segregation was legal as long as blacks and whites had equal facilities. The majority of whites had accepted segregation, but most blacks had not. They knew that separate was not equal. It meant inferior treatment, schools, and facilities for African Americans.

In large part due to the efforts of civil rights activist A. Philip Randolph, President Truman in 1950 signed an executive order to integrate the Armed Forces. Then, in 1954, the United States Supreme Court outlawed segregation in public schools. The following year, schools across the country were ordered to integrate as soon as possible. Many southern states resisted the order for as long as they could. In fact, they resisted many aspects of integration.

An incident in 1955 became one of the most important events in what now is known as the civil rights movement. Rosa Parks, a seamstress in Montgomery, Alabama, broke the law: She refused to give her seat in the front of a city bus to a white person. She was arrested for her action. In response, the Reverend Martin Luther King, Jr., organized a boycott of city buses. Eventually, laws granting preferential seating to whites were overturned.

In his late twenties, Malcolm X became a rising star in the Nation of Islam.

King believed in nonviolent protests to achieve integration. His methods included staging sit-ins at lunch counters that refused to serve blacks, and holding mass rallies such as the March on Washington. Malcolm X, meanwhile, spoke of integration not only as unachievable but as unwanted. Instead, he sought a separation of the races.

"Segregation is a condition enforced by a superior on an inferior," he once said. "Separation is a mutual agreement between equals. The white man will never have any respect for the black man until they are separated from each other."[8] He was also once quoted as saying, "Coffee is the only thing I like integrated."[9]

Malcolm said that African Americans should obtain their civil rights by any means necessary. Many people thought this statement meant that Malcolm X advocated violence. "He advocated brotherhood," said his daughter Ilyasah.[10]

Malcolm attracted attention with his powerful, controversial statements. He also cut a striking figure. Malcolm was six feet five inches tall and slender. Like his mother, he had a light bronze complexion. He kept his reddish-tinged hair cut very short. He wore well-made, conservative suits and followed the strict Muslim codes of behavior.

With Malcolm's successes in Detroit, Boston, and Philadelphia, Muhammad had a new mission for Malcolm X. In 1956, Muhammad sent Malcolm to

Mosque No. 7 in Harlem. This was considered a very prestigious assignment, second only to the Nation of Islam's headquarters in Chicago.

Shortly after Malcolm arrived in Harlem, he crossed paths with the woman who would become his wife. Betty Sanders was in New York attending nursing school.

"I just noticed her, not with the slightest interest, you understand," Malcolm recalled in his autobiography. "For about the next year, I just noticed her. . . . She never would have dreamed I was even thinking about her. In fact, probably you couldn't have convinced her I even knew her name. It was Sister Betty X."[11]

4

MEETING
MALCOLM

etty Sanders did not immediately fall in love with Nation of Islam spokesman Malcolm X. Nor was her courtship with him traditional. She was a junior at Brooklyn State Hospital School of Nursing. One day, a friend invited Betty and a date to dinner. Afterward, at the friend's urging, they all attended a lecture at Mosque No. 7 in Harlem. Betty's friend was a member of the Nation of Islam. She wanted Betty to meet her minister. His name was Malcolm X.

"Just wait until you hear my minister talk," Betty's friend said. "He's very disciplined, he's good-looking, and all the sisters want him."[1]

Years later, Shabazz recalled that she was not enthusiastic about hearing Malcolm X speak. She was not familiar with his views. She also was afraid that her parents would not approve of Black Muslims, who seemed so different from the people who attended Bethel A.M.E. Church. However, she felt she owed it to her friend to listen to the lecture.[2]

Malcolm was not there that night, so Betty went again on another night. In an article for *Essence* magazine, she wrote about the first time she saw the man who had so impressed her friend.[3] Betty described Malcolm X as tall, thin, and important looking. She liked his clean-cut appearance and no-nonsense manner. She also approved of his message. That night, Malcolm spoke of having the courage to do the right thing.

Betty admired Malcolm X, but she did not plan on becoming a Black Muslim. So she did not return to Mosque No. 7. Then, a while later, Betty was invited to another friend's house for a dinner party. Malcolm was among the guests. He and Betty struck up a conversation. They spoke of Betty's experiences with racism in Alabama. These were feelings she had never explored before. For Betty, it was a new and gratifying experience.

"I remember my mother saying that it was her husband who was the first person who ever talked about it openly, the feelings that she had," Ilyasah Shabazz said. "It was my father who first articulated her feelings of racism, her feelings of being treated in a distinct manner because of her brown skin."[4]

After that dinner party, Betty began attending Malcolm's mosque to hear him speak. "He would actively seek me out, ask me questions," Betty recalled. "He was different. He was refreshing, but I never suspected that he thought of me in any way other than as a sister who was interested in the Movement. Besides, there were too many people in line for his affection."[5]

"He was just an awesome kind of guy," Betty said. "He was disciplined. He knew what he was going to do and if he said he was going to do it, he did it. And he had a certain kind of worldly maturity that women my age at the time just dreamed about."[6]

How did Malcolm feel about Betty? In his autobiography, Malcolm said that Betty's intelligence first attracted him. He also liked the fact that she was almost as tall as he was, and that she was eleven years younger. Elijah Muhammad had taught Malcolm that to be compatible partners, men and women should be of similar height. Muhammad also said that the woman should be younger than the man, and that the woman should treat the man as a figure of authority. These were guidelines that Malcolm kept in mind as he and Betty got to know each other.[7]

Later in 1956, Betty was persuaded to join the Nation of Islam. She became Sister Betty X. She and Malcolm did not date because Muslim rules forbade it.

Malcolm X was a fiery and passionate speaker, and he attracted attention with his controversial statements.

Instead, they went out in groups with other members of the Nation of Islam. Betty usually sat in the backseat of the car with the women, while Malcolm and the men sat in the front. As Malcolm drove, he and Betty exchanged glances and smiles in the rearview mirror. They went out to dinner or attended cultural events or lectures at other mosques.

"Malcolm treated me really special, but he treated everybody special," Betty recalled. "But what most attracted me to him was his nobility. He always made me feel very comfortable. If he said he was going to call, you could bank on it. If he said he was going to do something, you could be assured that it would be done. He did not play games."[8]

Malcolm X became a very important person in the Nation of Islam. He was Muhammad's most trusted assistant. Malcolm traveled widely and successfully organized mosques throughout the country. In 1957, Muhammad sent Malcolm to Los Angeles to organize an Islamic mosque there. Whenever Malcolm was in New York, he called on Betty.

Meanwhile, Betty continued to attend nursing school. She also lectured at the mosque on women's health issues. She was an instructor there on health and hygiene. During one summer break from school, Betty went to Detroit to visit her parents. The Malloys became concerned when Betty told them she was attending a Muslim mosque. At one point, they threatened to stop paying for her education unless she severed ties with the Nation of Islam.

Before she left New York, Malcolm had given Betty the telephone number of his brother Wesley, who lived in Detroit and was also a Black Muslim. Betty and Wesley became friends that summer. With others, they went to movies and out to dinner. After her summer break ended, Betty returned to New York. One day, she ran into Wesley, who was in town visiting Malcolm. Wesley told Betty that Malcolm said he was going to marry her. According to Betty, that was the first time she heard of Malcolm's plans.[9]

In January 1958, Malcolm traveled to Detroit on Nation of Islam business. While he was there, he telephoned Betty in New York. He asked her to come to Detroit so that they could get married. Malcolm had already told Muhammad of his plan to marry Betty, and Muhammad approved.

Betty left New York the next day to meet Malcolm in Detroit. She took Malcolm to her parents' house so that they could meet him. According to the article Betty later wrote for *Essence* magazine, the Malloys liked Malcolm—until Betty said they were engaged. Then her parents became upset.

The Malloys "were afraid" of Malcolm and Betty marrying, their daughter Gamilah-Lamumba Shabazz said. "When you're comfortable, you don't want to shake the boat. And that was tipping it over, I guess."[10]

"They didn't approve at all," Ilyasah Shabazz said. "They still loved her, but they didn't approve."[11]

Perhaps Malcolm was unaware of their feelings. He later wrote that the Malloys were surprised but happy for the couple.[12]

Betty spent the night at her parents' house. The next morning, Malcolm picked her up. They drove to Indiana, where they had heard a couple could get married without a waiting period. That was no longer true, so they got back in their car and drove to Lansing, Michigan. They took the required blood test and bought two wedding rings. Then they went to a courthouse and were married by a justice of the peace. Afterward, they went to Malcolm's brother Philbert's house for an impromptu wedding dinner.

Betty's parents may not have approved of the marriage, but other people did. Ella Collins, Malcolm's sister, had been worried that Malcolm was working too hard. "I was deeply concerned about his health," she said later, "and was glad that he now had someone nearby who would see that he ate and slept properly."[13]

There was no time for a honeymoon for the newlyweds. Betty had to return to school, and Malcolm had work to do. The day after they were married, Betty returned to New York for nursing classes. A few days later, she rejoined her new husband in Detroit, where Malcolm had stayed on Muslim business. After a few more days, Betty and Malcolm came back to New York

In 1958, Betty married Malcolm X and also earned her degree as a registered nurse.

together. They shared the news of their marriage with their fellow Muslims.

In 1958, Betty earned her certification as a registered nurse. In the Nation of Islam religion, a wife is expected to dress modestly and to serve as a wife and homemaker. She is not encouraged to be independent. Much as Betty wanted to work, a career would have to wait. Her first priority was to be Malcolm's wife and assist him in his efforts. Thus began a marriage that Betty once described as beautiful, unforgettable, and the greatest thing in her life. "I was so happy," Betty recalled. "I don't remember being that happy in my entire life."[14]

5

LIFE AS MRS. MALCOLM X

he newlyweds began married life sharing an apartment house in Queens, New York, with another Muslim couple. Malcolm traveled frequently on Nation of Islam business. He was organizing mosques all across the United States. As the number-one spokesman and minister for the Nation of Islam, he also represented Elijah Muhammad, the head of the Nation of Islam, in radio interviews and college appearances. Malcolm was a charismatic, powerful speaker.

In the six years since he had been released from prison, Malcolm had converted thousands of African

Americans with the message of the Nation of Islam. He had recruited young men and women throughout the country, including many from neglected communities and prisons. Their transformation from street youths to morally responsible citizens was impressive. They also had neat appearances, adopting the practice of wearing suits with white shirts and bow ties and cutting their hair very short.

The Nation of Islam was fairly well known in African-American communities. It was not until 1959, however, that the white community at large became aware of Malcolm X and the Black Muslims. That was the year that CBS-TV aired a documentary, *The Hate That Hate Produced*. In the program, newsman Mike Wallace referred to "the rise of black racism."[1]

With the cameras rolling, Malcolm repeated the stories that Muhammad had taught him: The white race was a race of devils, and hell was what African Americans endured on earth. Malcolm also warned of a global revolution by dark-skinned people, "a lake of fire, a day of slaughter . . . for this sinful white world."[2] The comments struck fear and unease in many whites and blacks alike.

Though Malcolm's words sounded harsh, he was vocalizing the frustrations of many African Americans of the time. Despite Supreme Court rulings, most public places in the South remained segregated. African Americans were often threatened or harmed when they tried to vote or exercise other civil rights. Justice was not found through the courts. Also, there were very few national African-American role models. The few television and movie actors of color were usually depicted in subservient, degrading roles. The times were ripe for Malcolm's fiery words. As he once said, "All Negroes are angry, and I am the angriest of all."[3]

Behind the powerful public figure was an equally powerful, yet quieter, presence: his wife, Betty. Sister Betty, as she was known, was the behind-the-scenes person who helped Malcolm stay focused and organized. She made all of his suits by hand.[4] She always kept an extra suitcase packed and ready for her husband. When Malcolm returned home, he traded his suitcase of dirty clothes for the suitcase Betty kept waiting for him. When Malcolm left for business, Betty laundered and folded his clothes, packed the suitcase, and had it ready for the next time her husband returned home.

Betty also handled hundreds of requests for interviews and information. Author Alex Haley, who helped Malcolm X write his autobiography, once said that he was impressed with the way Betty responded to the constantly ringing telephone. Haley recalled Malcolm phoning Betty from out of town for his messages. Then, Malcolm spent several minutes jotting down the information Betty had compiled in his absence.

Betty also understood Malcolm's need for space

and quiet time during the rare occasions he was home. "She's the only woman I ever even thought about loving," Malcolm wrote in his autobiography. "And she's one of the very few whom I have ever trusted."[5]

Malcolm also wrote that beauty and love were more than just physical. He said he loved Betty's behavior, attitude, thoughts, and disposition.

Aside from keeping track of Malcolm's schedule, Betty assumed the main responsibility for raising their family. The couple's first child, Attallah, was born in November 1958. Qubilah, another daughter, was born in 1960. Their third daughter, Ilyasah, was born in 1962.

Betty had come a long way from the eager-to-please girl she had been. She had defied her parents by marrying Malcolm, though they later reconciled to her choice. Now she was not afraid to stand up for her wishes and desires. Sometimes that led to conflict. For example, Betty wanted to work outside the home. She had worked hard to earn her nursing degree. She was volunteering at the mosques, but she was anxious to put her skills to use in a paying job. Malcolm, however, was firmly against it. In accordance with Nation of Islam teachings, the wife was to stay at home and devote her time to her husband and children. Betty was so upset over the issue that she walked out on her husband three times. She would go to Philadelphia where her biological father, Shelman Sanders, lived

Behind the powerful public figure of Malcolm X was an equally powerful, yet quieter, presence: his wife, Betty, pictured here with daughters Attallah and Qubilah.

with his wife, Madeline, and their three sons. "Each time I left he [Malcolm] found me, and I was always so happy to see him," she said.[6]

Despite the absences and the conflicts, there were many very loving and tender moments in Betty and Malcolm's marriage. Years later, their daughters recalled seeing them dancing together in the house. Public dancing was frowned upon in the Nation of Islam, but private moments such as these were allowed. Malcolm was no-nonsense and disciplined, yet quick to make his wife laugh with a witty story, Attallah once said.[7] Malcolm called his wife "Apple Brown Betty" or "Brown Sugar."

Betty also maintained her sense of independence. "Betty, at a time when women were subservient in the Nation of Islam, when women were supposed to be covered up, refused to do that," said her sister-in-law, Ameenah Omar. "She refused to look anything but beautiful. She was beautiful and she wanted to look that way. My husband [Philbert, Malcolm's brother] also said that Betty had a very strong streak of independence, that she was not going to refuse to say something because she was a woman or because she was Malcolm's wife. She still had her opinions, and she did not hesitate to share those opinions whenever she got the opportunity."[8]

As the 1950s gave way to the 1960s, social unrest in the United States began to grow. Civil rights marches in Alabama, Georgia, and other southern states turned violent as police officers used high-powered water hoses, clubs, and attack dogs on peaceful protesters.

"The black man at last can see what the white man is really like, what he really feels about him," Nation of Islam leader Elijah Muhammad told *Life* magazine in 1963. "At last the black man realizes he must fight for his rights if he is to attain them."[9]

Those comments conflicted with the beliefs of another African-American civil rights leader. The Reverend Martin Luther King, Jr., supported peaceful, nonviolent protests, such as sit-ins and marches, to end segregation. In a sit-in, demonstrators would sit at racially segregated public places, such as lunch counters and bus stations. When they refused to leave, they would be arrested. The protesters welcomed the arrests to gain attention for their cause.

In 1963, King spoke at a rally in Washington, D.C. It drew hundreds of thousands of supporters of the civil rights movement. There, King delivered his celebrated "I Have a Dream" speech.

"I still have a dream," he said. "It is a dream deeply rooted in the American dream. I have a dream that one day this nation will rise up and live out the true meaning of its creed: 'We hold these truths to be self-evident: that all men are created equal.'"

"I have a dream that one day on the red hills of Georgia the sons of former slaves and the sons of former slave holders will be able to sit down together at the table of brotherhood."[10]

Malcolm X, too, dreamed of social justice and change, but at that time he believed in separation of the races. He preached on street corners and at Nation of Islam meetings. He spoke at college campuses and churches and in other countries, at university forums and broadcasting studios. "Justice now! Freedom now!

Dr. Martin Luther King, Jr., believed that civil rights protests should be peaceful, without violence.

Not when the white man feels he is finally ready to give it to us!" he said.[11]

Malcolm called Martin Luther King, Jr., and his African-Americans supporters "modern Uncle Toms" and "puppets of the white liberals."[12] "The white liberals have a guilt complex about the Negro," Malcolm said. "They love people like King who salve that guilt feeling a little. That's why they finance him. He's their darling. But when a Negro moves into a white neighborhood, who are the first to flee? The white liberals every time. Negroes who think otherwise are blinding themselves to the facts."[13]

Malcolm also said the United States government should give a part of the country to African Americans so that they could live apart from white culture and white civilization. He continued to make inflammatory remarks about white people, condemning their ongoing social injustices.

By 1963, a conservative Republican senator named Barry Goldwater had become the most requested speaker at college campuses in the United States. But Malcolm X was the second most requested speaker. He was also becoming more important in the Black Muslim and civil rights movements. Muhammad, the leader of the group, was in poor health. In May 1963, he asked Malcolm to go to Washington, D.C., to spread the word of Islam. Malcolm also continued as head of the Harlem mosque, and as its business manager.

Malcolm X shares a special moment with his young daughters
Attallah and Qubilah.

While Malcolm was in Washington, Betty and the children stayed in New York. By then, Malcolm and Betty and their children had moved to a small brick bungalow in East Elmhurst, Queens. The house had been bought by Muhammad, who provided housing as payment for Malcolm's hard work.

In Washington, Malcolm held nightly meetings. He recruited young African Americans who were headed for trouble. He also harshly attacked white America.[14]

Malcolm was accustomed to dissent from society at large. However, he was not prepared for conflict within his own Muslim community. Yet it happened in November 1963. President John F. Kennedy was assassinated in Dallas, Texas. Malcolm X used that opportunity to speak out once again. This time, it set into motion events that would soon lead to another tragedy.

6

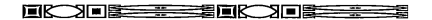

ASSASSINATION

n November 22, 1963, President John F. Kennedy was shot and killed. He had been riding in an open car in Dallas, Texas. The president's death marked the first American political assassination of modern times. Unfortunately, it was the first of several in the turbulent 1960s.

Kennedy, who was forty-three when he took office, was the youngest man ever to be elected president of the United States. He and his wife, Jacqueline, were very popular with the public. They were considered elegant, stylish, and charming. The president's death, at age forty-six, was a great shock. Most Americans reacted to the news of his death with overwhelming grief and horror. For three days, television stations provided round-the-clock coverage of the tragedy.

Hours after the assassination, Nation of Islam leader Elijah Muhammad contacted Malcolm X and other Muslim ministers. He ordered them to not make any comments about Kennedy's death. A few days later, Malcolm spoke at the Manhattan Center in New York. The title of his speech was "God's Judgment on White America." It had been planned before Kennedy was killed.

After Malcolm spoke, someone asked his opinion of the president's assassination. Malcolm said he thought it was an example of the "chickens coming home to roost." This expression means that past actions lead to future consequences. Malcolm later wrote in his autobiography that he used the expression to mean that hatred in white America now affected white people, too. Before, it had affected only black people.

The news media reported Malcolm's statement. The American public was horrified and outraged. Many believed Malcolm had been disrespectful to the beloved president. They also believed he was condoning violence. Newspaper editorials condemned Malcolm for speaking out.

Muhammad responded by suspending Malcolm X from his duties. Malcolm was not allowed to speak publicly for ninety days. He was not allowed to preach even at Mosque No. 7.

At first, Malcolm accepted the suspension. Soon, however, he began to believe that Muhammad was trying to permanently silence him. He also believed that this action had little to do with his statement about Kennedy's death. Earlier, Malcolm had discovered that Muhammad was unfaithful to his wife. Malcolm also learned of financial wrongdoings. Years later, Betty said Muhammad feared being exposed by Malcolm. So Muhammad wanted to distance himself from Malcolm and to have others shun Malcolm, too.

Also, Muhammad was very ill, and Malcolm was considered his most likely successor. Some members of Muhammad's family were jealous. They expected to take over after Muhammad's death.[1]

Malcolm quickly became disillusioned with the Nation of Islam movement. He needed a break. In January 1964, Malcolm took Betty and their three daughters to Miami, Florida. At the time, Betty was pregnant with their fourth daughter, Gamilah-Lamumba, who would be born later that year. This was the family's first vacation together. As it turned out, it would also be their last.

Malcolm and Betty were in Florida at the invitation of boxing champion Cassius Clay. The boxer, who later became known as Muhammad Ali, was a Black Muslim. He had been converted by Malcolm. The two men had become very close friends. After this visit, however, their friendship ended. Clay remained loyal to Elijah Muhammad.

Malcolm was able to relax a little in Florida. He also spent time thinking about his future. Malcolm believed Elijah Muhammad would find an excuse to restrict him further. Malcolm later said that Betty was a great source of comfort during this period.[2] He leaned on her, and she supported him emotionally.

Malcolm X with boxing champion Muhammad Ali a few days after Ali won the 1964 World Boxing Association title.

After they returned from vacation, Malcolm decided to make a pilgrimage to Mecca. A pilgrimage is a journey to a holy place. Mecca, in Saudi Arabia near the Red Sea, is the holiest city of Islam. There, Malcolm met Muslims of many different colors. He discovered that Elijah Muhammad's teachings did not follow orthodox Islamic ways. True Muslims did not believe that the white race was a race of devils. That had been Muhammad's own interpretation. And true Muslims did not embrace Elijah Muhammad as the messenger.

"In the land of Muhammad and the land of Abraham, I had been blessed by Allah with a new insight into the true religion of Islam and a better understanding of America's entire racial dilemma," Malcolm wrote in letters to Betty and to his sister Ella.[3]

Malcolm also traveled to Africa and the Middle East. He came back to the United States a new man. He was eventually given the name El-Hajj Malik El-Shabazz. It meant "rebirth." Malcolm and Betty both became Sunni, or orthodox, Muslims. Betty was now known as Betty Shabazz.

Malcolm realized his antiwhite statements had led to more problems between the races. He announced that he would stop making negative comments about white people. He also told civil rights leader James Farmer that he was ready to work with white people to achieve civil rights. The "old" Malcolm would never have agreed to that.

In March 1964, Malcolm officially left the Nation of Islam. Louis X, who would later be known as Louis Farrakhan, became spokesman for the Nation of Islam. Meanwhile, Malcolm started a new group, called Muslim Mosque, Inc. Some of Muhammad's followers left the Nation of Islam to join Malcolm. He said it was not an antiwhite group but a pro-black group. "I want to take Negroes out of the ghetto and put them in good neighborhoods in good houses," he said. "We've got to get rid of drunkenness, drug addiction, prostitution and all that."[4]

Malcolm then established a black nationalistic movement with freedom, justice, and equality as goals. He called it the Organization of Afro-American Unity. He softened his views and statements against white people. However, he still spoke powerfully for black equality. Many people thought he promoted violence. But Malcolm said he was misunderstood. He simply believed African Americans should defend themselves.

"I don't believe in passive resistance," he said. "Every Negro ought to have a weapon in his house—a rifle or a shotgun. Any Negro who is attacked should fight back; if necessary, he should be prepared to die like a man, like Patrick Henry."[5]

"Any Negro leader must be prepared," he added, "and must tell the people who are following him to prepare—to go either to jail, the hospital or the cemetery. But not without a fight, not without a reason."[6]

Friday 9 AM—April 25, 1964

Dear Alex Haley:

I have just completed my pilgrimage (Hajj) to the Holy City of Mecca, the Holiest city in Islam, which is absolutely forbidden for non-believers even to rest their eyes upon. There were over 200,000 pilgrims there, at the same time. This pilgrimage is to the Muslim, as important as is going to "Heaven" to the Christian. I doubt if there have been more than ten Americans to ever make this pilgrimage. I know of only two others who have actually made the Hajj (and both of them are West Indian). Mr. Muhammad and two of his sons made what is known as "Omra" (the pilgrimage or "visit" to Mecca outside of the Hajj season). I think I'm the first American born Negro to make the actual Hajj ... and if I'm not the

First page of a letter from Mecca by Malcolm X to Alex Haley.

After visiting the holy city of Mecca, Malcolm X sent this letter to author Alex Haley, who was helping to write *The Autobiography of Malcolm X*.

Malcolm also said, "I am not for or against violence. I am for freedom, by whatever means necessary."[7]

Malcolm was later credited with inspiring the change from the term *Negro* to *black*. "Negro is the wrong word," Malcolm said. "It does not have any scientific meaning."[8]

During 1964, Malcolm also spoke out against African Americans' fighting in the Vietnam War. The war was growing more and more controversial. The majority of Americans did not understand why the United States was involved in the war. They did not support risking American lives. Also, many of the injured and killed were African Americans.

Men were usually exempt from the draft if they were in college. At the time, a higher percentage of whites than blacks attended college. That meant more African-American men were drafted to fight in the war. They also tended to serve in lower-ranking positions, because officer positions typically required a college education.

"If [Martin Luther] King . . . can tell Negroes to boycott buses . . . I see no reason why they cannot boycott the Army, Navy and Air Force," Malcolm said. "I don't think any Negro should fight for anything that does not produce for him what it produces for others. Whenever a Negro fights for 'democracy,' he's fighting for something he has not got, never had and never will have."[9]

Throughout his public life, Malcolm was compared to Martin Luther King, Jr. Both men sought better lives for their people, but their methods were different, and they were viewed differently by others. Malcolm X was feared and often misunderstood during his lifetime. Later, historians credited Malcolm X with inspiring the positive aspects of the Black Power movement. At the time, however, the most famous African-American was Martin Luther King, Jr.

Malcolm was facing problems with some of his former followers. Those who were still loyal to Muhammad drove by Malcolm's house. They taunted his family and made death threats over the phone. Malcolm told more than one journalist that he expected someone would try to kill him. Malcolm was insulted publicly. "Only those who wish to be led to hell, or to their doom, will follow Malcolm," Farrakhan wrote in a Nation of Islam publication. "The die is set, and Malcolm shall not escape. . . . Such a man as Malcolm is worthy of death."[10]

Meanwhile, Malcolm continued working on his autobiography, which he began when he was a follower of Muhammad. Malcolm wanted to rewrite portions of the book that described his troubled youth and his mistaken beliefs about whites. However, he decided to leave them alone, so that his record of false starts might inspire others.[11]

Malcolm also continued to speak publicly. He drew

new followers, including some who had not embraced the religion of the Nation of Islam but who now could align with Malcolm. He spoke for all oppressed people, including poor whites and women. "I know that societies often have killed the people who have helped to change those societies," he said. "And if I can die having brought any light, having exposed any meaningful truths that will help to destroy the racist cancer that is malignant in the body of America—then, all of the credit is due to Allah. Only the mistakes have been mine."[12]

Betty had supported her husband's new mission. Yet she and others were worried about him. "I was among those close to Malcolm, including Betty, who wanted him to take a breather from the struggle and focus for a while on himself and his family," his sister Ella said. "I urged him to . . . build up his financial situation so he could better take care of his family and his [new organization]. After totally devoting over ten years of his life to the struggle for human rights, there were times he was so broke he couldn't even afford a suit."[13]

In early 1965, Muhammad tried to evict Malcolm and Betty from their home in East Elmhurst. He claimed he never intended for them to keep it. Malcolm vowed to fight the eviction. He had not made much money while working as a Muslim minister. "He had given Elijah Muhammad all the money he made on behalf of the Nation of Islam," said his daughter Ilyasah.[14] The house was practically the only thing of value he had. It gave his family a sense of security.

Then, on February 13, 1965, in the middle of the night, two firebombs were thrown into a front window of Malcolm and Betty's house. Malcolm awoke just in time, and he managed to get Betty and their four young daughters safely out the back door. No one was hurt, but there was a lot of damage.

Malcolm and Betty did not have insurance. To add to their woes, the new minister of Mosque No. 7 accused Malcolm of setting the fire to get publicity. Betty was

In February 1965, two firebombs were thrown into a front window of the Shabazz home, above. Fortunately, Betty, Malcolm, and their four small daughters escaped without harm.

very upset. "I couldn't imagine anybody being that cruel," she later wrote. "I couldn't imagine that anyone who claimed to love Black people could do something like that."[15] Betty and the children temporarily moved in with a family friend. Malcolm, fearing for his family's safety, checked into a hotel. The local police force received a tip that Malcolm's life was in danger.

A few days after the fire, Malcolm and Betty went house hunting. Later, Malcolm told Betty he was sorry for all the troubles he had brought to the family. He loved her and the children, and he wanted to spend more time with them. It was one of the last tender moments of their marriage.

On February 21, 1965, eight days after their home was firebombed, Malcolm X went to the Audubon Ballroom in Harlem, New York. He was scheduled to speak at 2:00 P.M., but he never had the chance. Shortly after he came out onstage, he was shot and killed. Betty and her children were witnesses to the horrible event.

"We talked about what happened after Malcolm was assassinated," Betty's friend Laura Ross Brown said. "I know that she was devastated. . . . She didn't know where she was going or how she was going to live or what was going to happen to her. She had four little children and she was pregnant with twins, and that was, I think, one of the most devastating predicaments for a mother to find herself in."[16]

7

SINGLE MOTHER

olice officers were standing guard outside the Audubon Ballroom the day Malcolm X was killed. When they heard gunshots, they rushed inside. One suspect was captured. In the confusion, the other gunmen got away.

A friend took the Shabazz children home to wait. Someone ran to a nearby hospital and brought back a stretcher. Malcolm was lifted onto it and carried to the emergency room. Betty Shabazz and some others accompanied him. But it was too late for the doctors to do anything. Malcolm was dead on arrival.

Shabazz was devastated, but there was grim work

ahead. First, she had to officially identify her husband's body. That occurred the following morning at the medical examiner's office. A crowd of reporters waited for Shabazz. After the official identification, Shabazz spoke to them. She told the reporters that for weeks Malcolm had been saying someone was going to kill him. Even though he had been offered protection, "No one believed what he said," Shabazz said. "They [the police] never took him seriously, even after the bombing of our home, they said he did it himself!"[1]

As upset as she was, Shabazz had to take care of her children, who had been traumatized by the experience of seeing their father shot. "I was really impressed with and proud of the way Betty handled the children that evening," Malcolm's sister Ella Collins said, "especially the way she soothed them."[2]

Shabazz also made the funeral arrangements. Several funeral homes and churches in Harlem refused to let her hold services. They were afraid of possible violence. Finally, the Unity Funeral Home agreed to help. Betty asked that her husband's body be placed on view for three days.

Meanwhile, unrest did happen in the community. Mosque No. 7, Malcolm's former temple, was fire-bombed. A few days later, a mosque in San Francisco was bombed.

Police stepped up patrols around Harlem. They also posted guards at the funeral home. There, Malcolm's body rested in a bronze coffin covered with glass. A floral arrangement was placed atop his coffin. The card attached said, "To El-Hajj Malik, from Betty." During the viewing period, more than twenty thousand people paid their respects. The funeral home received bomb threats every day.

Actor Ossie Davis, a friend of Malcolm's, delivered the eulogy at the funeral. He called Malcolm "our manhood, our living, black manhood" and said that in honoring him, blacks honored what was best in themselves.[3] Betty Shabazz was escorted to the coffin. She kissed the glass as a final farewell to her husband. After the service, Malcolm's body was driven to Ferncliff Cemetery in Westchester County, New York. He was buried while Muslim prayers were spoken.

Coincidentally, a Black Muslim convention had been scheduled for the day before Malcolm's funeral. About twenty-five hundred people gathered in Chicago for that event. It turned into a public denouncement of Malcolm. Two of Malcolm's own brothers, Philbert and Wilfred, spoke publicly against him. So did boxer Muhammad Ali. The three Black Muslim men, despite their personal ties to Malcolm, had remained loyal to Nation of Islam leader Elijah Muhammad. "They were convinced to speak against him, and they later regretted it," said Malcolm's daughter Ilyasah.[4]

Elijah Muhammad himself spoke. "We did not want to kill Malcolm and we didn't try to," he said. "It was

□□□

Betty Shabazz mourns at the burial of her husband, Malcolm X.

his foolishness, ignorance, and his preachings that brought him to his death."[5] He also said, "Malcolm got what he was preaching."[6]

After Malcolm's burial, Betty Shabazz continued to worry about her family's safety. She put away most of Malcolm's notes, letters, and papers. She did not want her husband's enemies to use this information against him.

Eventually, three Black Muslim men were arrested and sent to prison for Malcolm's murder. Some people believed that justice had not been fully served. Civil rights leader James Farmer said there might be international ties to Malcolm's assassination. Shabazz herself thought others were involved and that Malcolm's death was part of a larger conspiracy. At one point, she said she believed the Central Intelligence Agency (CIA) was connected to it.[7] Her feelings and comments would have severe consequences in the future.

Shabazz became a widow when she was thirty years old. She faced life without her partner, and as a single mother to Attallah, Qubilah, Ilyasah, and Gamilah-Lamumba. Attallah, the oldest, was only six years old. Gamilah-Lamumba, the baby, was ten months old. Shabazz also had recently learned she was pregnant again. Seven months after Malcolm's death, she gave birth to twins, Malikah and Malaak. These girls would have no memories of their famous father.

For several weeks after Malcolm's funeral, Shabazz suffered from stress. She had trouble sleeping at night. She kept reliving the horror over and over in her mind: the sounds of gunshots, her children crying in terror, the screaming and shouting, the sight of her husband's body pierced with bullet holes.[8]

She also had little public support, from either whites or blacks. *The New York Times* published an editorial about Malcolm's murder. They called him "a twisted man" who turned "true gifts to evil purpose."[9] Carl Rowan, an African American who later became a columnist for *The Washington Post,* dismissed Malcolm as "an ex-convict, ex-dope peddler who became a racial fanatic."[10] Another writer called him "the symbol of violence and the spokesman for the violent 'Black Man' in America."[11]

At first, the Shabazz family was treated warily by "upwardly mobile blacks," according to journalist Lawrence Otis Graham, a neighbor who attended private school with Attallah and Qubilah Shabazz.[12]

Shabazz found strength and courage after a *hajj*, or pilgrimage, to Mecca in Saudi Arabia. Malcolm had taken a similar trip in 1964. He returned refreshed and renewed, with a new vision of himself and his mission. Malcolm had been planning to embark on another *hajj* with two doctors. The doctors asked Shabazz to take her husband's place. Remembering how it had transformed Malcolm, Betty Shabazz decided to go.

In 1965, Betty Shabazz found her life turned upside down. How
would she face life without her partner?

When she returned from Mecca, she was ready to go forward without Malcolm.

Later, she said that the *hajj* had helped her come to terms with the tragedy. "I learned that I had to adopt a personality of positiveness and high humor," Shabazz

A pilgrimage to Mecca, above, kindled the strength and courage Shabazz needed to raise six small daughters on her own.

said. "For, if I laughed, they [her children] laughed. . . . I learned that I couldn't even express sadness around them. I didn't want them to worry."[13]

Shabazz and her daughters stayed temporarily in a hotel suite in Queens, New York. Later, with royalty payments from her husband's autobiography, she bought a home in Mount Vernon, New York. She spent the next several years living quietly and raising her six children. The family received some financial help from private donations. Actors such as Sidney Poitier and Ruby Dee held fund-raising parties in the family's honor. Shabazz also made ends meet by working as a nurse when she could. Nevertheless, the family struggled financially.

Eventually, Shabazz discovered that she wanted to continue her husband's work. She would begin by furthering her own education. "She understood my father's vision," Gamilah-Lamumba Shabazz said years later. "She understood African Americans as intelligent, articulate people. She understood the system."[14]

"She understood that she had to live and raise her children," Gamilah-Lamumba added. "She understood that if she in any way took on my father's [public] role, that that would mean death. So I guess she sat down one day and said, 'How can I do this?' And education was a vehicle for that."[15]

In the early 1970s, Shabazz began attending college classes. She earned a bachelor's degree in public health administration, and a master's degree in early childhood education, from Jersey City State College in New Jersey. A housekeeper watched Shabazz's six daughters while their mother studied. The girls kept very busy. Ilyasah Shabazz and her sister Gamilah-Lamumba recalled lessons in ballet, tap, drama, piano, and Arabic, among others.

"Our days were totally full, booked," Gamilah-Lamumba said. "But we weren't brats. My mother wanted to make sure that we knew there were pitfalls ahead, and that we were able to handle them."[16]

"She was extremely cautious and overprotective, very stern, very loving," Ilyasah said. "She didn't let you know that she was pained. She didn't let her children know that. She tried to surround us with a lot of activity and love and happiness. She didn't want us to feel the pain that she felt."[17]

"She also had a strong work ethic," Ilyasah said. "She believed that we had a purpose in life and that life was not to be wasted, that you should always be doing something constructive." According to Ilyasah, their mother immediately dismissed complaints of not having anything to do. "There's no such thing as being bored," Betty would say. "Read a book."[18]

"There were no excuses we could make," Ilyasah said, "because despite everything, she was able to persevere, accomplish, succeed."[19] Shabazz also was health conscious. "We were the only kids in school with shredded carrots in our tuna fish sandwiches," Gamilah-Lamumba said.[20] She also recalled her mother preparing from scratch healthy snacks similar to granola and trail mixes.

Ilyasah had fond memories of the family's quality time together. "Every Sunday she took us to mosque," she said. "Immediately after, we'd have lunch together. When we would come home, she would wash our hair. And then she would do all six of our heads, in braids or barrettes. She went to the University of Massachusetts in Amherst for school, Monday to Wednesday, for her Ph.D. Housekeepers took care of us throughout the week."[21]

The family also went out to dinner on Thursdays at a local diner. "We thought it was a [fancy] restaurant," Ilyasah said with a laugh. "We didn't know that we didn't have a lot of money. You wouldn't have known. My mother was financially prudent."[22]

Shabazz also gave her children a strong sense of identity. "From day one, I knew who my father was," said Gamilah-Lamumba, who was not even a year old when he died. "His picture was everywhere. And she always talked about him, and in the present tense, so it was like he was there."[23]

The Shabazz girls were raised during the height of the Black Power movement of the late 1960s. The Civil Rights Act of 1964 outlawed segregation. Yet people's attitudes were slow to change. The Black Power movement evolved to bring about that change. Political and social organizations were formed for African Americans. Pride in black culture was emphasized.

There also was a downside to the movement. Riots broke out in some cities. More than thirty people died after a 1965 riot in the Watts section of Los Angeles, California. Several other clashes, some of which were deadly, occurred between African-American citizens and white police officers in the 1960s.

In 1968, Betty Shabazz attended a memorial program in Harlem. It marked the third anniversary of Malcolm X's death. Some of the speakers said some very harsh things about race. To some of the listeners, Malcolm's words seemed tame in comparison.

After finishing her master's degree, Shabazz began studying for a doctoral degree at the University of Massachusetts in Amherst. "Absolutely nothing could prevent my mother from completing what she set out to do," said Ilyasah Shabazz. "She would drive her Oldsmobile to Massachusetts [for classes], then come home and do the work. I remember her spread out on the living room floor, writing papers."[24]

"I am not for women having typical female roles," Betty Shabazz once said. "When my husband lived, that was the role I played. When he was assassinated, I had to do everything. If I didn't make the money and bring the food in and [pay the bills], we didn't eat, we didn't sleep, and we didn't have a house."[25]

In 1975, ten years after her husband's death, Shabazz received a Ph.D. degree in education administration. Her children were older, and Shabazz was ready to finally take up where her husband left off. She was ready to begin a career outside the home, and to continue to spread Malcolm's message.

8

SPREADING
THE WORD

n 1976, Betty Shabazz went to work for
Medgar Evers College, a campus of the City
University of New York in Brooklyn. The
college was named after a 1960s African-American
civil rights activist. Medgar Evers was shot and killed in
front of his home in Mississippi in 1963. His murderer
was a white supremacist, a person who believes whites
are superior. The killer was not convicted of the crime
until almost thirty years later. Evers's widow, Myrlie
Evers-Williams, continued to speak out for civil rights.
Eventually, she became head of the National
Association for the Advancement of Colored People

(NAACP). In February 1995, she was elected to her current position as chairman of the National Board of Directors of the NAACP.

Shabazz became close friends with Evers. She also became close to Coretta Scott King, the widow of Martin Luther King, Jr. Shabazz, Evers, and King all knew the pain of losing their husbands to assassins. They also felt the responsibility of continuing their husbands' legacies.

The three women occasionally took trips together. These offered them opportunities to share their sorrow, and to share laughs and good times as well. Betty, in particular, loved to learn new dance steps and make her friends giggle with her stories.

"We talked about what was in our hearts," Evers-Williams recalled years later, "things that we could not share with the public. And there were times when we just threw out everything and just became girlfriends."[1]

"I was speaking to Coretta King and Myrlie Evers recently," Betty's daughter Gamilah-Lamumba Shabazz recalled. "I said, 'All of your husbands within a ten-year period . . . shocked the world. And then it was over. But for thirty-three years, you women have carried on the struggle, triple the time they have.' The power and strength of these women are incredible."[2]

Shabazz worked at Medgar Evers College for twenty-one years. She started as associate professor of health administration. Later she became director of the

Department of Communications and Public Relations, and then, director of institutional advancement and public affairs. In this position, she helped to raise money for scholarships, activities, programs, and books for the school.

Shabazz became more involved with her community. She was an active volunteer with Jack and Jill of America Incorporated. This national group was formed in 1938 in Philadelphia, Pennsylvania. Its original purpose was to provide social opportunities for upper-class African-American families. Later, it added programs to prepare African-American children to become leaders in society. Jack and Jill volunteers also raise money to combat sickle-cell anemia and other diseases that primarily affect African Americans. The group sponsors tutoring sessions, scholarships, and leadership-training programs for African-American students.

Shabazz was also a member of Links, a national organization for African-American women. Her daughter Ilyasah was a member, too. The group, which was founded in 1946, supports social and charitable causes. According to Ilyasah Shabazz, her mother was one of the founders of the Greater Hudson Valley chapter of Links. Betty Shabazz served as national director of international trends and services for two years at Links. Patricia Russell McCloud, the national president of Links, described Shabazz as being organized and having good ideas, recalled Ilyasah.[3]

DR. BETTY SHABAZZ
Director of Institutional Advancement
and Public Affairs/Cultural Attache

MEDGAR EVERS COLLEGE
of the
City University of New York

1650 BEDFORD AVENUE
BROOKLYN, NY 11225
718: 270-4991

Shabazz worked at Medgar Evers College for twenty-one years.

"My mother was involved in anything that improved the quality of life," Ilyasah said. "She was involved in anything that was constructive and fun."[4] That included becoming an enthusiastic participant in the Mount Vernon Bowling League.

Shabazz's influence spread. She served as a volunteer presidential adviser on civil rights issues, race relations, and children's issues to Gerald Ford (1974–1977), Jimmy Carter (1977–1981), and Bill Clinton (1992–2000).

Shabazz was also an unofficial adviser to her daughters and their friends. "My mother was struggling to raise six, but if someone needed help, she'd take them in or give them advice," Ilyasah said. "It was always, 'Call my mother, she'll tell you what to do.'"[5] Shabazz developed a reputation for seeking out young African-American women and encouraging them, particularly in their careers. She also stressed the importance of a quality education. "She did not do this for recognition but because she had a desire to help," said Ilyasah.[6]

Betty Shabazz enjoyed dressing up and socializing. She and several friends started a gourmet club as a way to keep in touch and try new recipes. She attended dinner dances, and loved to eat out at her favorite restaurants.

Shabazz spoke at high school and college graduation ceremonies at predominately African-American schools. Everywhere she went, she explained her husband's message. Malcolm had been misunderstood, she said. His primary goal was African-American empowerment. He believed black people could, and should, stand up for themselves.

"Why should White people be running all the stores in our community?" Malcolm once said. "Why should White people be running all the banks of our community? Why should the economy of our community be in the hands of the White man?"[7]

"Our people have to be made to see that any time you take your dollar out of your community and spend it in a community where you don't live, the community where you live will get poorer and poorer and the community where you spend your money will get richer and richer," Malcolm said. "Then you wonder why where you live is always a slum area."[8]

Gradually, more and more people became interested in learning about Malcolm X. Betty Shabazz shared the legacy of her husband with the world. She helped transform his reputation into that of a man who stood for unity and pride. In the process, she became a familiar and loving figure in the African-American community. "She was like a one-woman cheering squad for black America," said Cathy Hughes, president and chief executive officer of Radio One, Inc., the nation's largest radio broadcasting company targeting African American listeners.[9]

"After meeting her and listening to her speak, you can't help but love her," recalled one woman. Another said, "When a lot of us had an opportunity to meet Sister Betty, it was like an opportunity to say thank you—thank you for your gifts to the world."[10]

"She looked for the good, found the good and celebrated that," said Edison O. Jackson, president of Medgar Evers College. "She used education as her vehicle of transformation."[11]

In the 1980s, a group in Omaha, Nebraska, formed the Malcolm X Memorial Foundation. The goal was to raise money for a memorial to Malcolm, who was born in Omaha. Malcolm's brother Wilfred supported the group. Wilfred had spoken against Malcolm at the time of his murder. Later, Wilfred had a change of heart and left the Nation of Islam. He told reporters that Malcolm had died as a believer in brotherhood and equality.[12] Betty Shabazz also worked to get a high school in Newark, New Jersey, named after her husband. In addition, she helped to establish the Malcolm X Medical Scholarship at Columbia University. In turn, recipients would have to make a contribution to the improvement of health issues in African-American communities and the broader society.

In 1983, Shabazz began hosting her own radio talk show. She started at WBLS-FM in New York City. During the next several years, she hosted shows at other black-oriented stations, including WLIB-AM. At this station, Shabazz's show was called *A Forum for Women*, and it aired on Thursdays. Shabazz opened her program with Chaka Khan's song "I'm Every Woman." As the song played, Shabazz was often "grooving and singing in her seat," recalled her daughter Gamilah-Lamumba.[13]

On the show, Betty Shabazz interviewed a variety of local, national, and international figures—authors, activists, business leaders, celebrities, heads of state. "On my radio program I deal with topics I think young people or people who are trying to find their way might enjoy. I might talk about new career openings or options for women . . . [who] must make decisions for themselves and for their families," she once said.[14]

Betty Shabazz helped the world see Malcolm X as a man who
stood for unity and pride. Historians now credit him with
inspiring the positive aspects of the Black Power movement.

"Dr. Shabazz used her program to educate women and men on how to use resources available to them. She made sure that guests left the audience with issues to think about and critically examine," said Cynthia Smith, producer of Shabazz's program at WLIB Radio.[15] Issues discussed included education, health, and politics.

Gamilah-Lamumba Shabazz worked with her mother at one station for two years. Gamilah-Lamumba looked back on those years as very special. Her mother showed her love in many ways. One day, Betty walked up to her daughter's desk, tossed a small package on it, and walked away. Gamilah-Lamumba opened the present. Inside were a gold ring and earrings shaped like a star and decorated with an X.

"We both have short, fat hands," Gamilah-Lamumba recalled with a laugh. "My mother said that my father used to say, 'Betty, you are the beautifulest woman on earth but your feet and your hands, good Lord!'"[16]

Said daughter Ilyasah, "My mother expressed her emotions freely with me. She lived with certain standards and expected the same from her children. She had individual and distinct relationships with each daughter."[17]

On the twentieth anniversary of Malcolm's death, Betty Shabazz spoke to a writer for *Essence* magazine.

Shabazz said she did not usually grant interviews because she wanted to be considered a supporter, not a leader. However, she felt it was important that she continue to spread Malcolm's message. "He was a man who . . . uncovered an unjust system and saw examples of it around the world and wanted to bring an end to it," Shabazz said. "He felt that if we were going to have a world where brotherhood exists, then all people were going to have to work together."[18]

In 1986, an opera was produced based on Malcolm's life. Shabazz attended the opening. Four years later, a national group of supporters proclaimed 1990 as the Year of Malcolm X. Twenty-five years had passed since Malcolm's death. The group wanted to honor his memory by publicizing his message. The movement gained momentum. Rap artists used sound bites from Malcolm's speeches on their albums. Authors wrote books exploring Malcolm's message. T-shirts and baseball hats with "X" on them appeared everywhere. Sales of *The Autobiography of Malcolm X* rose significantly.

"There's something in Malcolm which touches the core of younger people," said Howard Dodson of the Schomburg Center for Research in Black Culture. "He was willing to stand up, to talk straight. Malcolm was a man—a real man."[19]

Yet Malcolm's appeal was not limited to younger people. Supreme Court Justice Clarence Thomas said

Malcolm X was his hero because Malcolm believed in blacks helping themselves. Thomas, an African American, was a controversial nominee to the Court because of his conservative beliefs and his opposition to affirmative-action programs.

"Malcomania," as one writer dubbed it, reached a high point after 1992. That is when filmmaker Spike Lee made a movie of Malcolm X's life. As a young African American, Lee wrote, directed, and produced movies such as *Do the Right Thing*, *She's Gotta Have It*, *Jungle Fever*, and *Summer of Sam*. Lee was in junior high school when he first read Malcolm's autobiography.

Lee said he made the movie *Malcolm X* in the hopes that young African Americans would "stop doing the crazy stuff we're doing. Stop killing each other." He called Malcolm's life incredible. "Here's a man who rose up from the dregs of society, spent time in jail, re-educated himself and through spiritual enlightenment, rose to the top."[20]

Lee's movie was filmed on location in New York, South Africa, Egypt, and Saudi Arabia. Angela Bassett portrayed Betty Shabazz. Al Freeman, Jr., played the role of Elijah Muhammad. Oscar-winning actor Denzel Washington starred as Malcolm. Washington had played Malcolm years earlier in an off-Broadway play called *When the Chickens Come Home to Roost*. Friends of Betty Shabazz went to the play. They told her they were impressed with how much Washington looked and sounded like Malcolm. Shabazz's friends urged her to see the play, but she refused. "At that time I could not afford emotionally to see it," she said.[21] Stronger now, Shabazz agreed to be a consultant to Lee's film. She reviewed his script and suggested some changes.

"I'm private," Shabazz said after the movie came out. "But there were some public things I had to do, because of [Malcolm's] commitment to the cause. I loved [Malcolm], and he loved the people."[22]

Lee ran into some problems while making the movie. The studio financing it, Warner Brothers, thought Lee was spending too much money. When Lee spent more than the budget, the studio cut off funding. Lee and Washington contributed most of their salaries to complete the movie. Lee also called on prominent African Americans to help finance it. Supporters included Oprah Winfrey, Bill Cosby, Michael Jordan, and Janet Jackson. Millions of dollars were raised. Lee said in an interview that by contacting African Americans, he was living up to Malcolm's message. "I'm tired of asking white folks, 'Please Mr. White Man, do this for me,'" Lee said. *"Do for self.* Black folks got plenty money."[23]

The renewed interest in and appreciation of Malcolm X brought some problems to the Shabazz family. Some people producing T-shirts, books, and other items with Malcolm's words and images had not obtained official permission. Shabazz grew concerned

Betty (played by Angela Bassett) and Malcolm (Denzel Washington) celebrate their wedding in the 1992 film *Malcolm X.*

that people were trying to get wealthy at the family's expense. "I woke up one morning . . . and thought, 'This is abuse in the broadest, deepest and wildest sense,'" Shabazz said. "'If I don't sleep, eat or anything else, this is going to end.'"[24]

Shabazz hired attorneys to ensure that her family was not taken advantage of. She later said that she wanted as many people as possible to learn about her husband. However, Shabazz wanted to maintain control over who was spreading his message. That was her right as Malcolm's widow.

"Her charming smile, easy manner, and kindly

spirit were not to be taken for granted by anyone, because she was a strong-willed person who demanded respect everywhere she went," said C. DeLores Tucker, founder of the National Political Congress of Black Women.[25]

In the 1990s, focus was also renewed on Malcolm X's killers. Three men had been convicted of the murder: Thomas 15X Johnson, Norman 3X Butler, and Talmadge Hayer. Hayer had been caught at the scene of the crime. He admitted his guilt. However, Hayer said Johnson and Butler were innocent. Hayer said he had four other helpers who had come from a black Muslim mosque in Newark, New Jersey. Louis Farrakhan had visited the mosque before Malcolm's murder. Farrakhan would go on to become leader of the Nation of Islam after Elijah Muhammad's death.

Butler served twenty-two years for a crime he said he did not commit. Many experts who studied the case also believed that both Butler and Johnson were innocent. "It's not conceivable that they were involved," said Peter Goldman, who studied the crime scene.[26] Goldman is a journalist and author of *The Death and Life of Malcolm X*. He said that Malcolm's aides would have known if Butler and Johnson had entered the ballroom that day. Shabazz, on the other hand, was not convinced that they were innocent. "They were there— they were recognized," she said in 1994.[27]

Ever since her husband's death, Shabazz had been doubtful that the crime had been completely solved. In 1994, the usually private woman agreed to be interviewed on WNBC-TV's *News Forum*. During the interview, Shabazz publicly stated that she thought Farrakhan had been involved in the murder of Malcolm. Later, she would regret speaking so publicly.

9

FAMILY TROUBLES

hose who knew her said Betty Shabazz was a devoted mother who raised her daughters well. She stressed education, independence, and heritage. She "was our everything," said her daughter Gamilah-Lamumba Shabazz.

As in most families, the Shabazz daughters have some differing memories of their childhoods. "She kind of raised us separately because we always clashed," said Gamilah-Lamumba. "But that's [common] in any family, so I have no problems with expressing it. All us girls have strong, strong minds."[1] Gamilah-Lamumba became a poet and rap artist. She often incorporates quotes from her father into her songs.

Ilyasah Shabazz said, "We had excellent and full childhoods at camps in Vermont, charm school, music, everything together. I cannot recall ever clashing as children or adolescents. If anything, we may have had differences after our mother's demise; we were older, living independently."[2] Ilyasah, with a degree in biology and a master's degree in education, had several jobs in education and the entertainment industry before taking a position as the director of public relations for the city of Mount Vernon, New York.

Attallah Shabazz, the oldest, works as an actress, producer, and writer. She often lectures about her father to corporate groups. Malikah Shabazz became an architect, and Malaak is a computer programmer.

Despite Betty's Shabazz's firm and loving guidance, not all of her children were able to overcome the traumatic memories of their earliest years. Perhaps the one most affected was Qubilah. The second oldest, Qubilah was almost five years old when she witnessed her father's murder. A family friend recalled that after the shooting, Qubilah was the only child who seemed to understand that her father was never coming back. "I was always angry he left me behind," she said later. "If he were a simple store clerk, he would still be here."[3]

Qubilah was quiet, intelligent, and sensitive. "I watched from a friendly distance as Betty's children grew up, achieved success, and, in the case of her seemingly cursed daughter Qubilah, fell apart," wrote journalist Lawrence Otis Graham.[4]

Like her sisters, Qubilah attended private schools. She graduated from the exclusive United Nations International School in New York City in 1978. After high school, Qubilah enrolled at prestigious Princeton University in New Jersey. She had difficulty adjusting. Graham, who also attended Princeton, said many white students avoided Qubilah. They feared that she shared the antiwhite sentiments her father had once expressed. Other students treated her like a celebrity, Graham said. They liked pointing out her dormitory room to campus visitors, recalled Graham. "A third group of people who should have been Qubilah's natural allies probably created the most damage of all," Graham said. "These were blacks who admired Malcolm X and resented the shy, dignified Qubilah for lacking the fiery, militant personality they expected from his child."[5]

Qubilah left Princeton after one semester. She returned for a semester the following year, and then quit altogether. In 1980, she moved to Paris, France. She took classes at the Sorbonne. Fluent in French and Arabic, she worked as a language tutor and translator for an electrical-engineering firm. In 1984, she gave birth to Shabazz's first grandchild. She named the baby Malcolm after her own father. Qubilah did not reveal the identity of the baby's father to her family. He is said to be an Algerian man she had met in Paris.

A few months after Malcolm's birth, Qubilah took him back to the United States. She and her son first settled in Los Angeles. Then they moved from apartment to apartment, in cities from coast to coast, trying to find a place where they belonged. They spent time in California, New York City, and Philadelphia. Qubilah held a series of low-paying jobs. She struggled to make ends meet. Her family feared that she was emotionally unstable. They also thought she might be using drugs or alcohol.[6] Their fears grew as the years passed.

Qubilah and Malcolm returned to New York in 1992, shortly after Spike Lee's movie about Malcolm X had arrived in theaters. Their lives continued to be unsettled. "I saw a sister of mine tonight and she was worried . . . about my son," Qubilah told a friend in 1994. "My family is very—they find my character to be a bit suspect," she added. "And they think they can do a much better job of raising my son."[7]

Qubilah's problems made it difficult for her to care for young Malcolm. In the summer of 1994, she decided to place the nine-year-old boy in a hospital for emotionally troubled children. He also spent time away from his mother, staying in the homes of relatives, where he behaved well.[8] "His mother could not take care of him, so the family extended themselves as all American families do," said his aunt Ilyasah.[9]

During this period, Louis Farrakhan and the Nation of Islam frequently made headlines. No one was quite sure how many followers the group had. "Those who know don't say. Those who say don't know," said the Nation of Islam's New York leader.[10] He was quoting a line often used by Malcolm X.

Malcolm X and the Nation of Islam had won praise for helping convicts "get straight," organizing street patrols, and finding employment for former drug abusers and homeless people. Farrakhan was getting publicity of a different kind. He had made many public comments against whites, Jews, and Catholics.

For many years, Qubilah Shabazz had harbored bad feelings toward Farrakhan. She held the group, and Farrakhan in particular, responsible for Malcolm's death. In January 1994, Betty Shabazz had been interviewed by *New York Newsday*. She told a reporter that she disliked Farrakhan. She also said Black Muslims were not real Muslims and that the group was not a real religion. The Nation of Islam's primary goal is to "maintain black people," she said. "My husband was about progress—and not just for African Americans but for all oppressed people. No one ethnic group is all bad and no one ethnic group is all good. I have good friends—from all backgrounds—all over the world."[11]

In March 1994, Farrakhan gave a speech. He said he was not involved in Malcolm's murder. He did admit that his harsh words may have spurred others to act. A few days later, Betty Shabazz told a television reporter that she still believed Farrakhan had been involved in the shooting.[12]

Until then, Qubilah had never spoken publicly about her father. Indeed, she had never discussed him with her close friends. But two months after her mother's TV interview, Qubilah renewed an acquaintance with a former high school classmate from the United Nations International School. She began talking to Michael Fitzpatrick on the telephone. Fitzpatrick had a shady past. He was addicted to drugs and alcohol. He also had financial problems. At the time, he was living in Minneapolis, Minnesota.

Qubilah later said she fell in love with Fitzpatrick. Over the telephone, the two formed a plan to kill Farrakhan. Qubilah said she was worried for her mother's safety. Betty Shabazz had been so open about accusing Farrakhan. Qubilah worried that someone would try to kill Betty.[13]

In the fall of 1994, Qubilah and Malcolm moved to Minneapolis. Qubilah told friends that she and Fitzpatrick were getting married. Qubilah found an apartment and enrolled Malcolm in school. She and Fitzpatrick briefly discussed the plan to kill Farrakhan.

After a few weeks, Qubilah said she changed her mind about the plot. She tried to contact Fitzpatrick but could not reach him. Qubilah also was having problems with raising Malcolm. He was removed from her care because of suspicions that he was being neglected.[14]

Shortly before Christmas in 1994, Qubilah was visited by agents from the Federal Bureau of Investigation (FBI). She was told that Fitzpatrick was an informant for the FBI, and that he had been taping his telephone conversations with Qubilah. In January 1995, Qubilah was charged with plotting to kill Farrakhan to avenge her father's death.

The African-American community's response was swift and loud. Betty Shabazz and others said that Qubilah had been set up—that she had been manipulated and trapped by government agents. They said that Fitzpatrick, who is white, was trying to avoid prosecution on drug charges. Even Farrakhan, the target of the assassination plot, came to Qubilah's defense. He said the government had used Qubilah in its attempts to silence him. Farrakhan helped Shabazz raise money for her daughter's legal expenses. "I'm most appreciative of Mr. Farrakhan—and surprised—his words, his patience, his generosity," Shabazz said.[15]

Others were suspicious of Farrakhan's motives. "It's disgusting," said the Reverend Charles Keyatta, who was assaulted in the 1960s and blamed it on Black Muslims. "It's all designed to bring respectability to Farrakhan. He knows he can never replace Malcolm as a leader if he doesn't make some kind of concession to the family for what he did."[16]

"But he didn't," said Ilyasah Shabazz, "and it became a publicity spoof. It was extremely difficult for my mother, but she agreed for the sake of her daughter and for unifying Blacks."[17]

Qubilah faced ninety years in prison and a $2 million fine. Then, shortly before her trial was to begin, her lawyers made a deal with prosecutors. Qubilah agreed to get psychological counseling and substance-abuse treatment. The charges reportedly would be dropped if she successfully completed these programs.

"If it were not for my mother, I don't think I would have held up at all," Qubilah said. "She acted more or less as a buffer for the whole nasty situation. She absorbed a lot of the pain for me. She called the [legal] shots all the time."[18]

Later in 1995, Shabazz traveled to Washington, D.C., to join Farrakhan's Million Man March. She went "not because of Farrakhan but for the significance of men uniting," said her daughter Ilyasah. "I went with her."[19] Farrakhan had asked African-American men to gather in the nation's capital in a show of unity and pride. Shabazz helped organize a women's program to coincide with the march. Other women organizers included poet Maya Angelou and civil rights pioneer Rosa Parks.

After her plea bargain, Qubilah moved to Texas for treatment. Seeking anonymity, she changed her name. She also got a job at a radio station. Malcolm, meanwhile, was sent to live with Shabazz in New York. He called his grandmother "Mommy Betty."

In 1997, Qubilah successfully completed counseling and substance-abuse treatment. Finally, her life seemed to be coming together. She resigned from the radio station with the hopes of opening a clothing shop. She also got married. That year, after a two-year separation, Malcolm returned to his mother in Texas.

Young Malcolm had blossomed under Betty's care. He attended school regularly and seemed to be happy. Now he was looking forward to living with his mother and having a father figure in his life. Malcolm made friends quickly at the private school he attended. "He didn't wear a big X on his T-shirt," the school principal said. "He was just Malcolm."[20]

Sadly, things fell apart once again. Qubilah and her husband separated. She brought assault charges against him. Malcolm was being neglected, and he began missing school. He also began lashing out at his mother. Qubilah twice called the police to say that Malcolm had hurt her. After one call, both mother and son were sent to a hospital for psychological treatment.

Qubilah's life was spiraling downward once again. And once again, Betty Shabazz came to her daughter's aid. Shabazz told Qubilah to send Malcolm back to live with her. Mommy Betty would take care of him. Qubilah needed to focus on getting her life together.

Shabazz was now sixty-three years old. She was done raising children. But Malcolm, twelve years old, needed her desperately. "She knew that she was his last hope and his best hope," said Ernest Davis, a longtime friend of Shabazz's and mayor of Mount Vernon, New York. "She was from the generation that still believed that you have to invest in children and sacrifice for them."[21]

Betty Shabazz's decision was made out of love and concern. It would end up costing her dearly.

10

THE MESSAGE LIVES ON

alcolm Shabazz moved in with his grandmother, Betty Shabazz, at the end of April 1997. The twelve-year-old boy had lived with Betty off and on throughout his turbulent life. "He was talking about how he was happy that he had this opportunity to go back to New York," said Charles Andrews, Jr.[1] Andrews was manager of the Texas radio station where Malcolm's mother, Qubilah Shabazz, had worked.

Yet shortly after Malcolm moved in with Shabazz, he was ready to leave. Betty got busy trying to find a school for her grandson. Malcolm, meanwhile, spoke of going back to be with his mother.

Betty Shabazz had raised six children of her own under difficult circumstances. She was an educated, vibrant woman. She had helped many other people with her kindness, hard work, and good deeds. She was respected and beloved. But in the end, even this woman could not ease the troubled mind of Malcolm Shabazz.

Betty's last official outing was on May 24, 1997, at Medgar Evers College. The occasion was a career development seminar and prayer breakfast for African-American women who had experienced physical and sexual abuse during childhood. Shabazz spoke movingly about her own idyllic childhood with the Malloys in Detroit and the lessons she had learned at Bethel A.M.E. Church. She advised listeners to encourage and support one another; to strive to change the world by changing themselves; and to have a plan for how they wanted to live their lives.

A week later, just after midnight on June 1, 1997, a fire broke out in the Yonkers, New York, apartment where Betty Shabazz lived. It started in the hallway outside her bedroom. Shabazz, dressed in her nightgown, woke up. She ran through the flames in an attempt to save her grandson. She suffered severe burns over most of her body. Shabazz was rushed to Jacobi Medical Center in the Bronx, New York. She was alive, but just barely. Her condition was extremely critical.

A few hours after the blaze, police found her grandson Malcolm wandering the streets. He smelled of gasoline. He admitted to police that he had set the fire. He said he wanted to return to his mother in Texas. Malcolm thought that if he caused enough trouble, Mommy Betty would send him back to live with Qubilah.

For a week after the blaze, Shabazz fought to survive. She underwent several painful operations to remove severely burned skin. Friends organized a blood drive to aid in her recovery. Thousands of people donated their blood at a Harlem bank. Prayer vigils were held. Well-wishers flooded the hospital with flowers, cards, letters, and telegrams.

Betty's oldest daughter, Attallah, spoke at a news conference at the hospital. She was accompanied by her five sisters. All six women wore purple ribbons to symbolize support for their mother as she struggled to live. Attallah said that the Shabazzes had never been a family to ask for anything, but "we are requesting your continuing prayer because she does hear it."[2] She also said that her mother was sometimes conscious, but she was unable to communicate with words. Her daughters whispered prayers in her ears.

"She went through five operations and the doctors took fat off of her stomach and back," Ilyasah, the third oldest, said later. "I told her, 'Mommy you've had a tummy tuck and a face lift. You're going to look great when you get out.'"[3]

Tragically, Shabazz lost the fight for her life. She

With their mother in critical condition, the six Shabazz daughters kept a vigil at the hospital. Standing, from left: Attallah, Qubilah, and Ilyasah. Seated, from left: Gamilah-Lamumba, Malikah, and Malaak.

died in the hospital on June 23, 1997, three weeks after the blaze. "Today America and the world has lost a champion of solid dignity and quiet strength," said the Reverend Jesse Jackson. "She never stopped giving and she never became cynical. She leaves today the legacy of one who epitomized hope and healing."[4]

Coretta Scott King said, "Her family has lost a mother, grandmother, and a sister. The nation has lost a committed civil and human rights activist whose life and contributions have made a significant difference."[5]

"My father lived strong, my mother did honorably, and her daughters are going to go through a lot in making this adjustment to living life without parents," Attallah said.[6]

"I just heard the news on the radio . . . and I stood still and prayed," one woman said. "It's painful and sad. She'd done so many good things for so many people. It's especially sad that her death could have been caused by her own grandson."[7]

The wake for Betty Shabazz was at Unity Funeral Home, the same place where her husband's had been held. Her coffin was copper, identical to his. A note from her daughters read, "To Mommy. Eternal Love, Your Six Daughters."[8] Many people of diverse ethnic backgrounds lined up to pay final respects.

The funeral was held at the Islamic Cultural Center in Manhattan. New York mayor Rudolph Giuliani and former boxing heavyweight champion Muhammad Ali were among the guests. Then Betty Shabazz was buried in a private ceremony at Ferncliff Cemetery in Westchester, New York. Her coffin was placed in the same plot where her husband, Malcolm X, was buried.

Two days later, a memorial service was held at Riverside Church in New York City. Thousands of people of all races, nationalities, and walks of life filled the pews and stood inside Riverside Church to listen to the speakers and honor Betty Shabazz. Outside, thousands more lined the street. They had come to pay their respects to a woman some of them had never even met.

The African Drums of Passion began the ceremony. The Boys Choir of Harlem sang "Kum Ba Yah" and "Wind Beneath My Wings." People from politicians to poet Maya Angelou and actors Ossie Davis and Ruby Dee were among those who spoke.

Betty's six daughters, Attallah, Qubilah, Ilyasah, Gamilah-Lamumba, Malikah, and Malaak, offered a moving tribute to their mother. "Where does one struggle to find language or vocabulary to be poetic or eloquent when it's something as pure and simple as 'Mommy'?" Attallah said.[9]

Malcolm Shabazz pleaded guilty to manslaughter and arson charges. His mother, Qubilah, attended the hearing. After his sentencing, Malcolm was sent to Hillcrest Educational Center in Lenox, Massachusetts. His minimum sentence was eighteen months. However, he could remain there for several years.

"I love him like he was my own child," said his aunt Ilyasah, with whom he often lived. "My feelings for him haven't changed. . . . He wanted to live with his mother and father and have a white picket fence, and he didn't understand why he didn't have the traditional American household as seen on TV or shared by his classmates."[10]

"We have to focus on Malcolm," Ilyasah added. "We have to make sure that he will be well, that he doesn't lose the rest of his childhood. My mother didn't want him to grow up in the [foster-care] system."[11] Ilyasah also said that Betty loved little Malcolm very much. "Had she survived," Ilyasah said, "still her primary concern would be Malcolm."[12]

Shabazz did not live to hear Louis Farrakhan admit his role in the murder of her husband, Malcolm X. On May 14, 2000, Shabazz's eldest daughter, Attallah Shabazz, sat across from Farrakhan on CBS-TV's *60 Minutes*. On national television, Farrakhan admitted to being a behind-the-scenes force that triggered her father's assassination. He said that he "may have been complicit in words that I spoke" that led to the killing.[13] Betty Shabazz had been right.

During her life, Shabazz received hundreds of awards. She volunteered her time for public and private organizations She also served on commissions and task forces at all levels of government as well as worldwide.

She was a member and active participant in the International Women's Conference in Beijing, China.

Shabazz set an example for single parents, African Americans, and women in particular. She was a role model for people of all races and nationalities. Betty Shabazz was a symbol of survival, strength, and courage. As her friend Myrlie Evers-Williams said, "[Betty] made a certain impact on a lot of lives, without a lot of fanfare. And she was so much more than Malcolm's widow."[14]

Shabazz was once asked about her personal philosophy of life. In response, she quoted her own mother. "My mother used to always say, 'You have to find the good and praise it.' A lot of us step over so much good, only to find that little bit that we can criticize."[15]

♦ ♦ ♦ ♦ ♦

On March 22, 1998, a largely African-American crowd gathered in Aaron Davis Hall at City College of New York. Many were dressed in brightly colored African garb. They called out greetings to one another while they waited for a dance performance by the Creative Outlet Dance Theatre of Brooklyn.

Afterward, to mark Women's History Month, a "Sheroes Among Us" reception honored several noteworthy women. They worked in the fields of religion, education, business, medicine, communications, the arts, and social change. The awards were sponsored by

Betty Shabazz was a role model for people of all races and nationalities.

4W Circle of Art. This Brooklyn organization works to keep African culture alive. It sponsors public events such as dance performances, and offers clothing and merchandise for sale.

During the awards ceremony, four women were singled out for the prestigious Spirit Award. This annual award is given to those who play a special role in reviving and enlivening the African-American community. Among the honorees was the late Dr. Betty Shabazz.

In the auditorium that night was Gamilah-Lamumba Shabazz. She had been scheduled to accept the award for her mother but had declined at the last minute. Her mother's death continued to leave her feeling unsettled. "At times, you just want to go hide," Gamilah-Lamumba said later. "It's going to take some time. The pressure is incredible."[16]

Yet Gamilah-Lamumba believed it was important for people to learn more about her mother and what she had accomplished. Indeed, it was not until Shabazz's death that her family discovered the full extent of her activities, Gamilah-Lamumba said.

"She was so private, she didn't always let her daughters know all that she did," Gamilah-Lamumba said. "Six girls [now] cannot handle what one woman did. I didn't realize the magnitude of it."[17]

"I knew because we spent a lot of time together as adults," said Ilyasah Shabazz. "She always let me know of her travels and contact number."[18]

Ilyasah also had planned to attend the ceremony. Then the family received a last-minute request to travel to Africa as part of President Bill Clinton's delegation there.

The trip was extra special, Ilyasah explained later, because her mother would have been going and had traveled to Africa many times prior. Betty Shabazz had been part of a delegation accompanying New York City mayor David Dinkins. "Before I knew it, I was on my way," Ilyasah recalled. "A friend of my mother's—Minyon Moore, a White House aide to President Clinton—told me, 'Your mother would be very proud of you, and I know she's smiling right now.'"[19]

Ilyasah recalled that when her mother had returned from her first trip to Africa, she cried as she told her daughter about it. Shabazz had been overwhelmed by the harsh conditions enforced on the indigenous people and still the warmth of the people. She also was saddened by the poverty she encountered.

"I was surprised [when she cried] because my mother, she was strong, she concealed the tears and the emotions," Ilyasah said. "The tears made her weak. And she knew she couldn't be weak to do what she had to get done. She shared her husband's legacy with us and contributed greatly."[20]

Indeed, Betty Shabazz remained strong until the end.

CHRONOLOGY

1934—Betty Sanders is born in Detroit, Michigan, on May 28; lives with her grandmother and aunt in Georgia.

1942—Moves to Detroit to live with her mother.

1946—Begins baby-sitting for Lorenzo and Helen Malloy; eventually they informally adopt her.

1952—Graduates from Northern High School; enters Tuskegee Institute in Alabama, intending to become a teacher, but decides she wants to study nursing instead.

1954—Becomes a student at the Brooklyn State Hospital School of Nursing in New York.

1956—Meets Malcolm X.

1958—Marries Malcolm X in January; earns nursing certification; daughter Attallah is born in November.

1960—Daughter Qubilah is born.

1962—Daughter Ilyasah is born.

1963—Malcolm is punished by the Nation of Islam for commenting on the assassination of President John F. Kennedy.

1964—Malcolm leaves Nation of Islam after making pilgrimage to Mecca; daughter Gamilah-Lamumba is born.

1965—Malcolm and Betty's home is firebombed; eight days later, on February 21, Malcolm is shot and killed in the Audubon Ballroom in Harlem, New York; twin daughters Malaak and Malikah are born seven months later.

1970—Betty returns to school, eventually earning a bachelor's degree in public health administration and master's degree in early childhood education from Jersey City State College in New Jersey.

1975—Earns doctoral degree in education administration from University of Massachusetts at Amherst.

1976—Begins a twenty-one-year career as an administrator at Medgar Evers College, City University of New York, in Brooklyn.

1983—Begins hosting a radio talk show.

1984—First grandson, named Malcolm, is born to daughter Qubilah.

1988—Second grandson, Malik AmjHaad, is born to daughter Gamilah-Lamumba.

1992—Serves as a consultant to Spike Lee's film *Malcolm X*.

1997—Shabazz dies three weeks after a fire in her apartment; grandson Malcolm is charged with setting the fire.

1998—Granddaughter, Betthi Bahiyah, is born to daughter Malikah.

Chapter Notes

Chapter 1. Suddenly Widowed

1. Malcolm X and Alex Haley, *The Autobiography of Malcolm X* (New York: Ballantine Books, 1992), p. 500.

2. "Tributes," *People Weekly*, December 29, 1997, p. 183.

3. Personal interview with Safiya Bendele, May 5, 1998.

4. Personal interview with Gamilah-Lamumba Shabazz, March 22, 1998.

5. Ibid.

Chapter 2. A Sheltered Childhood

1. Personal interview with Ilyasah Shabazz, April 6, 1998.

2. Ibid.

3. James Baldwin, "Letter from a Region in My Mind," *The New Yorker*, November 17, 1962, p. 95.

4. Dr. Betty Shabazz, "From the Detroit Riot to the Malcolm Summit," *Ebony*, November 1995, p. 62.

5. Personal interview with Gamilah-Lamumba Shabazz, March 22, 1998.

6. "Betty Shabazz," *Biography Today* (Detroit: Omnigraphics), vol. 7, no. 2, April 1998, p. 86.

7. Jamie Foster Brown, ed., *Betty Shabazz: A Sisterfriends' Tribute in Words and Pictures* (New York: Simon & Schuster, 1998), p. 31.

8. Ibid., pp. 31–32.

9. Shabazz, p. 64.

10. Personal interview with Ilyasah Shabazz.

11. Personal interview with Gamilah-Lamumba Shabazz.

12. Personal interview with Ilyasah Shabazz.

Chapter 3. Malcolm X

1. Malcolm X and Alex Haley, *The Autobiography of Malcolm X* (New York: Ballantine Books, 1992), p. 3.

2. Ibid., p. 13.

3. Peter Goldman, *The Death and Life of Malcolm X* (Chicago and Urbana: University of Illinois Press, 1974), p. 29.

4. Ibid.

5. Malcolm X and Haley, p. 126.

6. Ibid., pp. 234–235.

7. Goldman, p. 46.

8. Albert B. Southwick, "Malcolm X: The Charismatic Demagogue," *The Christian Century*, June 5, 1963, p. 740.

9. Goldman, p. 6.

10. Note to the author from Ilyasah Shabazz, April 7, 2000.

11. Malcolm X and Haley, p. 261.

Chapter 4. Meeting Malcolm

1. Betty Shabazz, as told to Susan L. Taylor and Audrey Edwards, "Loving and Losing Malcolm," *Essence*, February 1992, p. 52.

2. Ibid.

3. Ibid.

4. Personal interview with Ilyasah Shabazz, April 6, 1998.

5. Shabazz, Taylor, and Edwards, p. 54.

6. Robert D. McFadden, "Betty Shabazz, A Rights Voice, Dies of Burns," *The New York Times*, June 24, 1997, p. D20.

7. Malcolm X and Alex Haley, *The Autobiography of Malcolm X* (New York: Ballantine Books, 1992), pp. 263–264.

8. Shabazz, Taylor, and Edwards, p. 104.

9. Ibid.

10. Personal interview with Gamilah-Lamumba Shabazz, March 22, 1998.

11. Personal interview with Ilyasah Shabazz.

12. Malcolm X and Haley, p. 265.

13. Rodnell P. Collins with A. Peter Bailey, *Seventh Child: A Family Memoir of Malcolm X* (Secaucus, N.J.: Carol Publishing Group, 1998), pp. 96–97.

14. Shabazz, Taylor, and Edwards, p. 104.

Chapter 5. Life as Mrs. Malcolm X

1. Lewis Lord and Jeannye Thornton, "The Legacy of Malcolm X," *U.S. News and World Report*, November 23, 1992, p. 76.

2. Ibid., p. 77.

3. Malcolm X and Alex Haley, *The Autobiography of Malcolm X* (New York: Ballantine Books, 1992), p. 397.

4. Note to the author from Gamilah-Lamumba Shabazz, April 6, 2000.

5. Malcolm X and Haley, p. 267.

6. Betty Shabazz, as told to Susan L. Taylor and Audrey Edwards, "Loving and Losing Malcolm," *Essence*, February 1992, p. 109.

7. Charles Whitaker, "Who Was Malcolm X?" *Ebony*, February 1992, p. 124.

8. Jamie Foster Brown, ed., *Betty Shabazz: A Sisterfriends' Tribute in Words and Pictures* (New York: Simon & Schuster, 1998), p. 38.

9. Gordon Parks, "What Their Cry Means to Me—A Negro's Own Evaluation," *Life*, May 31, 1963, p. 78.

10. E. D. Hirsch Jr., Joseph F. Kett, and James Trefil, *The Dictionary of Cultural Literacy* (Boston: Houghton Mifflin, 1988), p. 268.

11. Parks, p. 32.

12. Albert B. Southwick, "Malcolm X: The Charismatic Demagogue," *The Christian Century*, June 4, 1963, p. 740.

13. Ibid.

14. Ibid.

Chapter 6. Assassination

1. Marc Crawford, "The Ominous Malcolm X Exits from the Muslims," *Life*, March 20, 1964, p. 40.

2. Malcolm X and Alex Haley, *The Autobiography of Malcolm X* (New York: Ballantine Books, 1992), p. 352.

3. Rodnell P. Collins with A. Peter Bailey, *Seventh Child: A Family Memoir of Malcolm X* (Secaucus, N.J.: Carol Publishing Group, 1998), p. 159.

4. "Now It's a Negro Drive for Segregation," *U.S. News and World Report*, March 30, 1964, p. 39.

5. Crawford, p. 40.

6. Ibid.

7. "Now It's a Negro Drive for Segregation," p. 39.

8. Ibid.

9. Crawford, p. 40.

10. M. A. Farber, "In the Name of the Father," *Vanity Fair*, June 1995, p. 59.

11. Thomas Kretz, S.J., "Criticism in the Christian World: Journey Toward Truth," *The Christian Century*, December 8, 1965, p. 1513.

12. Raymond A. Schroth, "Malcolm X Is Alive," *America*, April 22, 1967, p. 594.

13. Collins and Bailey, p. 180.

14. Note to the author from Ilyasah Shabazz, April 7, 2000.

15. Betty Shabazz, as told to Susan L. Taylor and Audrey Edwards, "Loving and Losing Malcolm," *Essence*, February 1992, p. 110.

16. Jamie Foster Brown, ed., *Betty Shabazz: A Sisterfriends' Tribute in Words and Pictures* (New York: Simon & Schuster, 1998), pp. 127–128.

Chapter 7. Single Mother

1. Malcolm X and Alex Haley, *The Autobiography of Malcolm X* (New York: Ballantine Books, 1992), p. 505.

2. Rodnell P. Collins with A. Peter Bailey, *Seventh Child: Malcolm X* (Secaucus, N.J.: Carol Publishing Group, 1998), p. 186.

3. Eldridge Cleaver, *Soul On Ice* (New York: Dell Publishing Co., 1968), p. 200.

4. Note to the author from Ilyasah Shabazz, April 7, 2000.

5. Peter Goldman, *The Death and Life of Malcolm X* (Chicago and Urbana: University of Illinois Press, 1974), p. 301.

6. Ibid., p. 302.

7. Ibid., p. 296.

8. Betty Shabazz, as told to Susan L. Taylor and Audrey Edwards, "Loving and Losing Malcolm," *Essence*, February 1992, p. 110.

9. Lewis Lord and Jeannye Thornton, "The Legacy of Malcolm X," *U.S. News and World Report*, November 23, 1992, p. 76.

10. "Now It's Negroes vs. Negroes in America's Racial Violence," *U.S. News and World Report*, March 8, 1965, p. 6.

11. C. Eric Lincoln, "The Meaning of Malcolm X," *The Christian Century*, April 7, 1965, p. 431.

12. Lawrence Otis Graham, "From Outcast to Heroine," *U.S. News and World Report*, June 16, 1997, p. 60.

13. Barbara Carlisle Bigalow, ed., *Contemporary Black Biography* (Detroit: Gale Research Incorporated, 1996), vol. 7, p. 246.

14. Personal interview with Gamilah-Lamumba Shabazz, March 22, 1998.

15. Ibid.

16. Ibid.

17. Personal interview with Ilyasah Shabazz, April 6, 1998.

18. Ibid.

19. Ibid.

20. Personal interview with Gamilah-Lamumba Shabazz.

21. Personal interview with Ilyasah Shabazz.

22. Ibid.

23. Personal interview with Gamilah-Lamumba Shabazz.

24. Personal interview with Ilyasah Shabazz.

25. Amy Alexander, *Fifty Black Women Who Changed America* (Secaucus, N.J.: Carol Publishing Group, 1999), p. 218.

Chapter 8. Spreading the Word

1. "Thousands Mourn Death of Dr. Betty Shabazz in New York City," *Jet*, July 14, 1997, p. 16.

2. Personal interview with Gamilah-Lamumba Shabazz, March 22, 1998.

3. Personal interview with Ilyasah Shabazz, April 6, 1998.

4. Ibid.

5. Ibid.

6. Note to the author from Ilyasah Shabazz, April 7, 2000.

7. "The Legacy of Malcolm X," *Ebony*, May 1989, p. 158.

8. Ibid., p. 160.

9. Jamie Foster Brown, ed., *Betty Shabazz: A Sisterfriends' Tribute in Words and Pictures* (New York: Simon & Schuster, 1998), p. 70.

10. Brenna Reilly, "Lexington Service to Honor Shabazz," *Lexington* [Kentucky] *Herald-Leader*, posted on the Internet.

11. Jim Fitzgerald, "Grandson Reportedly Set Fatal Fire," *Associated Press*, posted on the Internet, June 24, 1997.

12. "Brother Reveals Malcolm X Had Disavowed His Racist Philosophy in Later Life," *Jet*, June 10, 1985, p. 19.

13. Note to the author from Gamilah-Lamumba Shabazz, April 6, 2000.

14. Brian Lanker, *I Dream a World* (New York: Stewart, Tabori, & Chang, 1989).

15. Brown, p. 106.

16. Personal interview with Gamilah-Lamumba Shabazz.

17. Note to the author from Ilyasah Shabazz, March 10, 2000.

18. Joy Ducket Cain, "A Conversation with . . . Dr. Betty Shabazz," *Essence*, February 1985.

19. Vern E. Smith with Regina Elam, Andrew Murr, and Lynda Wright, "Rediscovering Malcolm X," *Newsweek*, February 26, 1990, p. 68.

20. "Denzel Washington Stars as 'Malcolm X' in Spike Lee Film," *Jet*, November 30, 1992, p. 39.

21. Laura B. Randolph, "Denzel Washington and the Making of Malcolm X," *Ebony*, December 1992, p. 126.

22. Robert D. McFadden, "Betty Shabazz, A Rights Voice, Dies of Burns," *The New York Times*, June 24, 1997, p. D20.

23. "Monument to Malcolm," *Vogue*, November 1992, p. 356.

24. James Bock, "King's Heirs Battle to Protect His Legacy," *The Baltimore Sun*, January 19, 1994, p. 1A.

25. Brown, p. 82.

26. Elaine Rivera, "The Disciple: Muslim Is Trying to Prove He Didn't Kill Malcolm X," *New York Newsday*, March 20, 1994, p. 8.

27. Ibid.

Chapter 9. Family Troubles

1. Personal interview with Gamilah-Lamumba Shabazz, March 22, 1998.

2. Note to the author from Ilyasah Shabazz, March 10, 2000.

3. Richard Lacayo, "The Troubles She's Seen," *Time*, June 16, 1997, p. 48.

4. Lawrence Otis Graham, "From Outcast to Heroine: A Family Friend Explores the Hard Life of Malcolm X's Widow," *U.S. News and World Report*, June 16, 1997, p. 60.

5. Graham, pp. 60–61.

6. Randy Furst, "Events Shattered Quiet Life Shabazz Would Prefer," *Star Tribune: Newspaper of the Twin Cities*, May 9, 1995, p. 1A.

7. Rachel L. Swarns, "Lost In Shadows of History; Shabazz Family's Troubles," *The New York Times*, June 8, 1997, p. B50.

8. Note to the author from Gamilah-Lamumba Shabazz, April 6, 2000.

9. Note to the author from Ilyasah Shabazz, March 10, 2000.

10. Michael H. Cottman, "State of the Nation: An Army of Muslims Stands Guard, Changes Lives," *New York Newsday*, January 30, 1994, p. 6.

11. Ibid.

12. Robert D. McFadden, "Betty Shabazz, A Rights Voice, Dies of Burns," *The New York Times*, June 24, 1997, p. D20.

13. Ibid.

14. Swarns, p. 50.

15. Ellis Henican, "Strange Bedfellows on Stage at Apollo," *New York Newsday,* May 2, 1995, p. A4.

16. Ibid.

17. Note to the author from Ilyasah Shabazz, March 10, 2000.

18. Furst, p. 1A.

19. Note to the author from Ilyasah Shabazz, March 10, 2000.

20. Lacayo, p. 49.

21. Bill Hewitt, "Legacy of Pain," *People Weekly,* June 16, 1997, p. 44.

Chapter 10. The Message Lives On

1. Bill Hewitt, "Legacy of Pain," *People Weekly,* June 16, 1997, p. 47.

2. "Betty Shabazz's Daughters Thank the Public for Its Support as Mother Struggles to Live," *Jet,* June 23, 1997, p.12.

3. Monte Williams, "A Shabazz Daughter Learns to Cope After Loss," *The New York Times,* August 23, 1997, p. 28.

4. Jim Fitzgerald, "Grandson Reportedly Set Fatal Fire," *Associated Press,* posted on the Internet, June 24, 1997.

5. Ibid.

6. Robert D. McFadden, "Disputes and Legalism Are Put Aside as Friends and Family Grieve," *The New York Times,* June 24, 1997, p. D20.

7. Ibid.

8. Note to the author from Ilyasah Shabazz, April 7, 2000.

9. "Thousands Mourn Death of Dr. Betty Shabazz in New York City," *Jet,* July 14, 1997, p. 16.

10. Williams, p. 28.

11. Ibid.

12. "Daughter of Malcolm X and Dr. Betty Shabazz Recalls Moments with Dying Mother in Hospital," *Jet*, August 4, 1997, p. 33.

13. Louis Farrakhan on *60 Minutes*, CBS-TV, May 14, 2000.

14. Jamie Foster Brown, ed., *Betty Shabazz: A Sisterfriends' Tribute in Words and Pictures* (New York: Simon & Schuster, 1998), p. 17.

15. Memorial service program for Dr. Betty Shabazz, transcript courtesy Owensby & Company Communications, New York.

16. Personal interview with Gamilah-Lamumba Shabazz, March 22, 1998.

17. Ibid.

18. Note to the author from Ilyasah Shabazz, March 10, 2000.

19. Personal interview with Ilyasah Shabazz, April 6. 1998.

20. Ibid.

FURTHER READING

Alexander, Amy. *Fifty Black Women Who Changed America.* Secaucus, N.J.: Carol Publishing Group, 1999.

Brown, Jamie Foster, ed. *Betty Shabazz: A Sisterfriends' Tribute in Words and Pictures.* New York: Simon & Schuster, 1998.

Collins, Rodnell P. *Seventh Child: A Family Memoir of Malcolm X.* Secaucus, N.J.: Carol Publishing Group, 1998.

Farber, M. A. "In the Name of the Father." *Vanity Fair,* June 1995.

Goldman, Peter. *The Death and Life of Malcolm X.* Urbana: University of Illinois Press, 1979.

Harris, Laurie Lanzen, executive ed. "Betty Shabazz." *Biography Today.* Detroit: Omnigraphics, Inc., vol. 7, no. 2, April 1998.

Lord, Lewis and Jeannye Thornton. "The Legacy of Malcolm X." *U.S. News and World Report,* November 23, 1993.

Malcolm X and Alex Haley. *The Autobiography of Malcolm X.* New York: Ballantine Books, 1964; 1992.

Parks, Gordon. "What Their Cry Means to Me—A Negro's Own Evaluation." *Life,* May 31, 1963.

Shabazz, Betty, as told to Susan L. Taylor and Audrey Edwards. "Loving and Losing Malcolm." *Essence,* February 1992.

Shabazz, Betty. "From the Detroit Riot to the Malcolm Summit." *Ebony,* November 1995.

INTERNET ADDRESSES

<http://www.Coloredreflections.com/decades/
Decade.cfm?Dec=5&Typ=2&Sty=1&SID=92>

<http://mscd.edu/~mooreeb/BETTY.html>

<http://www.thefuturesite.com/wlkatz/bshabazz.html>

<http://www.brothermalcolm.net/bettyshabazz.html>

INDEX

Pages with photographs are in boldface type.